Thomas Boyajian

The American Missionaries and the Armenian Protestant Community

Thomas Boyajian

The American Missionaries and the Armenian Protestant Community

ISBN/EAN: 9783337289225

Printed in Europe, USA, Canada, Australia, Japan

Cover: Foto ©Lupo / pixelio.de

More available books at **www.hansebooks.com**

AN APPEAL

AGAINST THE POLICY OF THE AMERICAN MISSIONARIES AMONG THE ARMENIAN CHRISTIANS.

Read at a Special Meeting held in the City of New York, United States of America, in 1867.

IN presenting to this honoured assembly a condensed account of the existing differences between your Missionaries and the Armenian Protestant Churches, I fear that some of my hearers will not hesitate to think that we—the Armenian Protestants—after having received incalculable blessings from the American Christians through their missionaries, instead of expressing gratitude are demonstrating an unchristian spirit and evincing ingratitude and dissatisfaction. I beg, therefore, to say that such feelings do not exist either in the hearts of my brethren or myself; and I can assure this assembly that we have always considered the Christians of this country, as well as their missionaries, our most respected benefactors. Feeling that their desire is to spread the light of the truth in dark countries in a way they think best, we—as far as it concerns us—think it our bounden duty to point out to them their mistakes in policy and operation, that the light may be spread more and more, till the earth is filled with the knowledge of the glory of the Lord. We feel that we are in a condition to do this because of our better acquaintance with the peculiarities of the people, and our knowledge of the manner in which the policy of the missionaries is affecting them.

You have, Rev. Gentlemen, before you a person to deal with who will be very glad to receive your advice; if he is mistaken in one or in all points, nothing will give him more delight and pleasure than to be corrected; and, when he returns to his country, it will give him great satisfaction to communicate to his brethren the opinion formed by this assembly, after a careful investigation of the points under question. I firmly believe that the result of this would be a reconciliation of all parties.

I wish it to be understood plainly that, as far as I am concerned, I have not any personal interest in prosecuting this matter. If you give to my people a better education, after being a father of a few children there is no probability of my having any share in it. If you increase the salaries of those employed by your missionaries, it will be no advantage to me; I have long ago determined to live and die with my people. As to treatment, I confess that the missionaries, with few exceptions, have behaved towards me with kindness and regard before these questions were raised. Then what induces me to speak? It is because I am convinced that if we do not attempt to remedy the existing evils, there will be danger of a reaction in the work, which will cause great pain to all who love the kingdom of Christ.

Perhaps some of you will be inclined to ask, are these complaints general, or in some Churches only? I have little doubt my friend, Dr. Wood, will reply: "They are only in Constantinople and its vicinity." We all of us are liable to forget things that are past. If he, in his leisure hours, takes the trouble to look into the Missionary Reports of the last fifteen years (preserved, I believe, in the Mission House), perhaps he himself will be surprised to find complaints, here and there, now and then. If he carefully examines all these, he will discover that there have been complaints in nearly all the stations where the missionaries reside; and his surprise will be still greater when he finds that these grievances are almost all marked by their peculiarities; these were stopped either by dismissing the complainants, or, for their high esteem and love to the missionaries, they did not dispute with them further. The fire, however, is under the ashes. I had the opportunity of seeing many of the pastors, preachers, and members of different Churches; nearly all of them have some complaints, only they are unable to trace them to fundamental principles. And what is most remarkable is, that the most intelligent among them have the most complaints. But suppose these are few; are we to look at the cause and nature of the complaints, or at the number of the complainants? If we find that they have reason for dissatisfaction, shall we say, because the great mass of the people are ignorant, we need not, therefore, remove the cause? If there is a leak in a boat, and only a little water flows in through it, shall we say it is of no consequence, this small quantity of water cannot endanger the safety of the boat? Does the danger lie in the quantity of water, or in that small leak by which the water flows in? Is it not the wisest way to take every measure, as soon as possible, to stop the leak which threatens the safety of the boat? A few years ago they used to say, "Only Pastor Simon Utijian and his Church are dissatisfied with missionary policy;" after a short time the Church at Haskeuy, then the Churches at Constantinople. Finding the numbers of dissatisfied Churches were increasing, the missionaries began, for the comfort of the Christians in America (perhaps their own also) to use the collective term, "Constantinople and its vicinity," instead of enumerating the churches. Who can understand how many Churches they mean in these collective words? Perhaps more than ten Churches.

Suppose we find that these Churches have some ground for dissatisfaction; will you leave them in this condition simply because the policy of the Mission is such as it is? Ah! policy is a good thing when it is adapted for a desired end; but after all policy is not gospel; it is framed by a few short-sighted human beings. They may make a mistake, and, indeed, a great many mistakes. It is, therefore, our duty to give due attention to those who complain, and either to satisfy their demands or to convince them of their errors.

The Christians in this country have spared neither money nor men to plant these churches. Now I ask you, my Christian brethren, to spare a few hours or days to find out a remedy for these difficulties.

I shall now proceed to state, briefly, the principal points of complaints, at the same time submitting them to your consideration.

First, the Church organization. When the missionaries found themselves under the necessity of organizing the first Churches, I have no doubt that they then did whatever they thought best, sincerely and prayerfully; but they must have known that this arrangement could only be temporary. Now, the circumstances are changed; there are numerous Churches with their own pastors, and many congregations which will soon be formed into Churches. It is evident—at least, from the Protestant point of view—that the Church herself is endowed with the right to choose the form of her organization. The present condition of our Churches, in consequence of their organization, is such that they are entirely disconnected, and have no sympathy with each other; they are longing after such an organization as shall contain unity among all individual Churches in profession, practice, and discipline, without destroying the rights of each individual congregation. Any organization which does not contain this simple element will prove, not only a failure, but will offend those to whom we intend to preach the Gospel. All those who are acquainted with Church history are aware that an organization which is peculiar to the Occidental mind cannot be adapted to the Oriental mind. What is the cause that the Roman Catholic Church, which has become the dominant Church in the West, has not succeeded in spreading itself in the East? The Oriental mind has always an inclination on the side of a form of religion which contains in it some elements which unite the whole race together. The Roman Catholic missionaries, having learned this great lesson, have given permission to their converts to have their choice. By this wise toleration, they have gained, and are gaining, a great many converts.

I cannot see what advantage is to be gained from keeping our Churches in their present isolated condition, the unavoidable conse-quence of which must be alienation from one another. We have Congregationalist and Presbyterian missionaries, some of whom are very extreme in their views, and impart their notions to the Churches under their care. Some missionaries advocate re-baptism, while the others condemn it. Churches under the former re-baptize, while the Churches under the latter condemn, and sometimes even go so far as to threaten to have no communion with them. Another branch springs out and says, " You have no authority in your Church ; we prefer the Episcopalian form." A missionary preaches, it is said, dangerous doctrines in regard to the Holy Trinity and atonement; Churches under his care are leavened with his doctrines. All these things are done on the responsibility of the missionaries themselves ; the Church has not a legitimate voice at all in these matters, only it is passive, subject to their views. If doctrinal and denominational differences are a part of missionary work, and desirable too, it will come to pass very soon ; but for the present, while the Protestants in our country are so limited in number, is it wise to keep them in this isolated condition ? And besides, must we not consider the form of the Government under which they have to exist, and what denominational system will be most effective ?

The only way to secure this end is to have a general conference of the Churches there to confer together (having the missionaries also with them) on this subject ; if possible, to consult previously with emi-nent and experienced ministers both in America and Europe, to act prayerfully and carefully, keeping before them the sublimity of the task, remembering that they are laying a foundation on the firmness of which depends, in one sense, the temporal and eternal welfare of present and future generations. But the missionaries object to this plan by saying, " You have no railroads, and the Churches are distant from each other." Is there any hope of having railroads next year ? They say, moreover, " How can so many persons come together ?" If we cannot come now, . we shall not come at all, for the number of Churches increases every year. Then they say " You must first have local unions, then the general one." We want the general one in order to form an organiza-tion by the general consent of the Church ; but if we organize the local unions, that will at once be a form. Besides, we *have* already the local unions. Then they say, " You must continue some time in this state until you have learned how to manage affairs like this." If we are able to manage the local unions, why not a general one? After all, they say, "It is very expensive." If the matter is important for the safety of the Church, let us not spare the expense. If the Board is not able to pay, let us ask the other Christians to help us in this great work. In reply to this they say, "No, we cannot advise you to do this." The meaning of all this is very clear—that is to say, they wish us to remain in our present position.

Before quitting this portion of my subject, let me mention that it is neither desirable to give to our Churches a denominational name (as we have already adopted the name of "Evangelical Armenians"), nor to mould them into the exact form of one of your Churches here. The most important element is their union, and if you name them here Congregationalists or Presbyterians, Methodists or Episcopalians, we shall not care at all.

Secondly, the relation of the missionaries with our Churches. The assertion of the missionaries that "they have not any relation with us," is altogether absurd. They are working in our Churches and through our Churches. We are their co-operators in that happy work. It is evident from the state of the case that they have relation with us. The only difficulty is to define the exact limit of that relation. In consequence of this the missionaries exercise unlimited control over our Churches.

The missionaries are the authorized agents of the Board. The funds are entrusted to them, and they are responsible for them. In order to aid in the support of our Churches and schools, they give from this money to our pastors, preachers, &c. Hence their right is unquestionable to have a voice in those matters. On the other hand, we have Churches regular in all respects, only they are not able to support themselves entirely. We think that these Churches also have rights—rights which have their origin in Heaven—sacred rights.

When a missionary is labouring in a new field he has a perfect right to employ or dismiss his catechists, preachers, &c.; but when he organizes a Church, that Church at once assumes a new position; he gives her rights that she had not before, and he ought to acknowledge them. He must either not organize a Church, or, if he does so, he must acknowledge her position.

It is said that the policy of Home Missions is similar to that of Foreign Missions. I am not acquainted with the operations of the former, but one thing is very clear to me. The relation of the home missionaries with their Churches is very different to that of the foreign missionaries with their Churches. The Mission Church at home is immediately under the Church who supports her. The members of the Mission Church are, in one sense, the members of the Church that cares for them. It is the Church that labours in Mission Churches, and consequently she has the right to admit members and keep them in the Mission Churches, which are branches of the mother Church, the missionaries acting as mediums between them. But the foreign missionaries are not, in the full sense of the word, the agents of the Church, but of a society. The society, as a society, has no right to admit members. If a missionary ever acts in this direction, he cannot act as an agent of a society, but in virtue of his ministerial capacity ; consequently he cannot admit members into another Church, but can only organize an independent Church. As soon as he organizes a Church, this new Church stands on the same level as others. Whether she supports herself or not, it is morally out of the power of a missionary to keep her down. Here is the weak point of a Missionary Society. Perhaps that was the reason that our Lord gave the commission of evangelization to the Church herself, and not to any society.

In connexion with this I will mention the necessity of a Christian tribunal between the missionaries and ourselves. The missionaries are not subject to any court, they are neither the members of our Church, nor have they any ecclesiastical connexion with us. Neither you nor they think that they are infallible ; the Pope only has such a claim—fortunately under dispute. It very frequently happens that difficulties arise between the missionaries and the Church members, pastors, preachers, and Churches. In such cases the missionary is a party in the quarrel ; at the same time he is the judge, and that without jury. He dismisses the pastors, excommunicates the Church members, nullifies the acts of the Church councils, deprives a regular Church of many years' standing of all her rights, and pronounces her to be void of all her capacities as a Church. This the missionaries do without being responsible to any one. It is impossible to get the missionaries to hear an appeal against another one. If you bring even a serious charge against one of them, their answer uniformly is, "You are not good men ; of course he had good reason for acting as he did." The only way of reconciliation with a missionary is unconditional surrender, and once a person is pronounced by any missionary as a bad man he is regarded in that light by all the other missionaries.

In justice to the missionaries I must here remark that most of these difficulties belong rather to their policy than to personal matters. The private life of many of them is considered by us to be a Christian life, but, notwithstanding, they are liable to mistakes and to sin.

The third point of difference is the question of education.

Missionary work has two objects before it : the first and the greatest is the salvation of souls, and the second the civilization of the world. While all of us agree that the principal means by which these ends are to be gained is the simple preaching of the Gospel, yet none of us doubt that this must be accomplished through educated and prudent Christians. That is the reason *why you send out educated missionaries.* Some may object to this by saying, "Were the Apostles educated?" To this I reply, No. But God in his infinite mercy deemed it necessary to send to his Church, in her infancy, one thoroughly educated—the great Apostle Paul; and who knows how many more? The Apostles had advantages which we have not; they were inspired by the Holy Ghost to understand the Scriptures and to write the New Testament. For us education is necessary that we may understand what they have understood and taught; besides, the means by which God made known his truth to the human mind were different then to what they are now. He used to speak to the senses more than to the intellect; it was for this that He bestowed upon the Apostles and the Church at large the gift of languages and the power of working miracles. But now he speaks directly to the intellect; therefore, those who have to convey God's truth to others must have preparation for it.

The work of a missionary is a temporary one; he is in the field until he finds the Church capable to do the work herself, then he leaves that place for another one. But pastors and preachers are the permanent officers of the Church; they have to improve and enlighten the people under their charge, and raise them as high as the level of Christian civilization.

At the commencement of missionary work among our people the missionaries acknowledged the principle above referred to; accordingly they established a better educational system. Just now, when there is a great demand for educated Christian ministers, they have closed the Bebek Seminary, under Dr. Hamlin, and established three others much inferior to that, and graduates from these are settling as pastors in the new-born Churches. Some of the missionaries declare even that they "do not desire to have educated pastors," and that "they do not require more knowledge for the present." In reply, I say we must keep in our mind the people to whom the missionary effort is directed; they are not savages and heathens, but civilized Christian people, though ignorant and superstitious. Your missionaries are not going to teach them the fundamental truths of Christianity, for they know them; but all they need is reformation, and this can only be effected by giving them a better literature and a higher Christian education, for all the corruptions of the Armenian Church have been introduced through the ignorance of the clergy and the force of circumstances in which she has been placed. Shall we place these reformed Churches in the same position? It is true that the present pastors are more educated than the people under their charge, but what is the extent of their knowledge? It is not uncommon to hear many of our pastors and preachers preaching, Sabbath after Sabbath, nothing else but the errors of corrupted Churches. How can a congregation grow in knowledge when they hear nothing but lectures like this? I am aware some will say " that after many years' experience Dr. Hamlin's seminary was not found to answer the purpose for which it was intended ; the students, after receiving a good education and learning the English language, were not willing to leave Constantinople and be employed in missionary work, but sought some other employment by which they might get rich." It is true. But we must take into consideration all the circumstances connected with it. When the Bebek Seminary was established there were only a few Protestants in the capital. Owing to circumstances they were obliged to admit students without regard to their religious persuasion. Of course none of the missionaries could expect to employ all those young men in their work, yet many of them offered themselves to the missionaries, and they became their right hands in the time of severe persecution, when missionaries could not raise their little finger. It was these men who translated books, even the Bible, into modern language, and became pastors and teachers to preach and teach the truth, while many of your missionaries were not able to repeat correctly the alphabet of the language in which they intended to preach the Gospel. The other students, though they did not directly work with the missionaries, nevertheless were not lost to the cause. Many of them became ministers and teachers among the Armenians of the ancient Church. They kindled the light of the truth among their people ; and when we hear of the great reformation movement in that Church, the originators of it are these students mostly.

But in the year 1852 the majority of the students were Protestants, and from the interior of the country. There were about twenty-eight. Out of this number twenty-three entered into the work ; some of them died in it, four of them left, and the remainder are in the work up to this day. Knowledge does not prevent us from labouring for Christ ; if we love Him we love also His cause, and we labour for it.

It is said, " Those who have a high education require a higher salary." This is true. But equally true it is that they can do more than those who have not the same education. The union which is generally called " The Kharpoot Union " has a president, a graduate of Bebek Seminary—a man of a considerable amount of education. If he dies to-day the union will perish with him. What a deplorable state of things ! so many Churches to be dependent on the life of one man. Does not this show us what education can do?

But the missionaries say, " We educate you now a little ; when you are able to support educational establishments, then you may do as much as you like." Ah! Who will persuade the people to support education if your missionaries teach our pastors and teachers " that science is an injurious thing. You must only learn your Bible; that is all that you and your children need?" Many a time have I seen people, in observing the books in the missionaries' study, say, "One or two Bibles are quite enough; what will you do with so many Bibles?" supposing that all those books were Bibles.

Again, the missionaries, as a general rule, do not reach the minds of our people; though some of them after many years' experience and toil may succeed. In a great measure they fail from want of perfect knowledge of the language, customs, and the mode of convey-ing ideas to them. They come to us with the full blessings of Chris-tianity. If we have well-educated men, capable of understanding the language of the missionary, they can act as mediums for transferring their Christian thought and ideas to our people; and thus, on the one hand, your missionaries will become useful from the very commence-ment of their labours; on the other hand, our young men will occupy many important posts in our schools and Churches, and, having the rich literature of the English language at their disposal, they will be able to impart its useful contents to our people. There will not be any need of sending a silent missionary to fill the chair of a professorship in the so-called Theological Seminary of Marsovan or elsewhere; one of our number will fill this post without spending years in learning the language.

Infidelity and Popery are rapidly gaining ground in our country. The Christian ministers have to contend with them. But how? With the Bible? But many of our pastors do not understand even those parts of the Bible which are oftentimes attacked by infidels. And at this day there is not a single Protestant minister amongst us who can be compared with many learned Armenian Roman Catholic priests. Either you will have to educate us or to support your missionaries amongst us for centuries.

But some will say, perhaps, If we educate them they will oppose us, and discuss our policy. I cannot see any harm in this. It is much better to have co-operators who are intelligent, and openly express their opinion, than to have those who can only echo your sentiments. Why should we exclude persons from the work because they are educated? Would you do the same in America? What would be public opinion about it? Would they tolerate it? I believe not.

It has been said, " It needs longer time and more expense for a better education." In reply, I must say neither extra time nor expense are necessary; all that is needed is willingness to teach. The course of study at the Bebek Seminary was only four years; during this time the students were taught nearly every branch of mathematics, natural philosophy, metaphysics, moral science, geography, astronomy, logic, rhetoric, systematic and practical theology, evidences of Christianity, Church history, besides the English, Greek, Armenian, and sometimes Turkish languages, &c., &c. The principal of that seminary was thoroughly acquainted with our language, and his first care was to acquaint the students more or less with his own. He always employed the best Armenian teachers that could be found. But in Kharpoot they have none. In Marsovan, although they have one, he is not well acquainted with his own language. The new missionary, who is the principal of that seminary, does not yet speak our language; the students do not understand his; what can you expect from such a school?

The fourth point is the present economy.

Economy, no doubt, is very important in a work like this; but if you injure your work by pushing it too hard, then you will have to pay for it.

In this great work two different agencies are employed—foreign missionaries, and brethren from the country itself. These two are equally essential for the work.

You send the missionaries without being sure they will succeed in learning the language and accustoming themselves to the climate of the country; many times the result is a failure. Of course you do not expect any benefit from a missionary simply because he is in the field, but you send him in the hope that he will succeed.

During the last few years, for the sake of economy, your missionaries have begun to diminish the small salaries of those in their employment, saying "they cannot afford to pay so much;" in the meantime they send for new missionaries and increase their own salary.

If I am not mistaken, the highest salary that a pastor receives does not exceed one quarter of that of a missionary (not mentioning those who get only one-eighth). It is believed generally that a missionary lives in great self-denial. How can it be that the needs of these two classes of people are so widely different? Either the missionaries receive very large salaries, and consequently do not live as the Christians believe they do, or they starve the pastors by giving them such a small sum. My opinion inclines to the latter. Some of these pastors and others, after being in this work for many years, and becoming fathers of two to seven children, when they find their small salary diminished they leave the work, if they can obtain some other employment, in order to support their families. If not, they spend their life in distress, and other valuable young men seeing this shrink from the work. Thus they damage the cause by expelling from the work superior men and opening the door for inferior ones. It is true that those who gave themselves to the cause of Christ did so without any expectation of getting rich; but it was understood, and many times promised, that the missionaries would support them. If economy is really necessary, it is better to keep those who are already working, and not to invite new missionaries, whose coming and going will cost ten times more to the society, and who will not be useful before five years, provided every thing be favourable.

As to the self-supporting doctrine, undoubtedly it is most important for the existence of our Churches; but we must push it as far only as they can bear it—not compel the people to sell their very beds to pay for the expenses of their Churches, and give a fine opportunity for the missionaries to publish it in America that the people under their care do so much for Christ.

The missionaries are not able to decide how much a congregation can afford to pay for the support of their religious and school expenses, for they are not acquainted with the circumstances of the people. The Protestants are generally from the poorer classes, and their numbers are very small. They give already five times more than they used to give while in their former Church; they have just suffered a bitter persecution—they lost all they had, churches, schools, and even grave-yard; they are oftentimes taxed heavily on account of embracing this religion; besides, being many times out of work, they have to strive for the daily bread of their poor children with none to sympathize with them. How can such a people support their Church? It is not because they do not wish to do it, but actually they cannot. Instead of compelling this people to support their pastor, you had better dismiss one or two of the eight missionaries in Constantinople; that will not have a serious consequence. The missionaries say it is not for economy, but for the Churches that we do so. When they find the salaries of their pastors small, they venture to take it upon them to pay it. Are we going to teach the Churches to support their pastors as beggars? If we do, can we expect any time that a respectable Christian man would offer himself to the work of the ministry, except those who would seek it merely for their daily bread. But they say they must have self-denial. Very good. Do you expect to find more self-denial there than in this Christian land? Are not the ministers of this country good examples for us? Would you blame a minister here, who, when he finds himself unable to support his family with his salary, and cannot possibly get it increased, gives up the ministry for another occupation?

But the missionaries say that the pastors must live like the middle class of their people. I accept this, with only a slight modification : they must not live as the middle class of *their own* people, but like the middle class of *the* people at large. Protestants are generally very poor, but their middle classes are poorer still. I once inquired into the circumstances of the Protestants of a particular town, when to my surprise I found that the wealthiest among them were in debt about £40. One of the Constantinople Churches contains only seven families belonging to the town, and Mr. Washburn told me that there were applications to him for help from all the seven. Now what is the middle class of this community? Even if the pastors are content to remain in this condition, what can you expect of them? They are not able to get a book or a paper to increase their knowledge, how shall they be able to instruct and interest the people of their charge?

As a general rule when the pastors and preachers come together, the subject of their conversation is their extreme need.

Now the question comes again, Is it not better not to give them even their present amount of education, then there will be no need of books, papers, or even ink? I confess it would make a little difference, yet I know that all those cheap pastors and preachers, "for we have them," are also quite as dissatisfied with their means.

If pastors are necessary to a Church, we must give them a reasonable salary, and we must teach the Churches also to do the same.

This is a brief account of the difficulties between the missionaries and our Churches.

For my own part I determined long ago to work for Christ and for my people, at any rate as far as God helps me, and in peace and harmony with missionaries as far as I am able. I have worked more than ten years with them, and I have never been the one to quarrel with them. But for the sake of the general cause it is most desirable to bring these things to a speedy solution; either correct if there is any thing to be corrected, or convince the people. The leak must be stopped at any rate. This disaffection is like a contagious disease—it will pass very rapidly from one Church to another.

To conclude in one sentence. If you desire to see the work more prosperous and sure in its progress, help to unite the Churches, establish a sound and reasonable relation between your missionaries and your Churches out there on the healthful basis of missionary and Church rights, give a good education to promising Christian young men, employ them in this blessed work (for a short time) with less stinted means, and yet far more economically than for the support of a missionary. Then you will see, and that not many years hence, that the Churches will become self-supporting, not for a short time only, as is now too often the case, but permanently, and they will assume an independent and manly spirit and position; and by their moral, spiritual, and mental light, under the grace of God, they will be able to enlighten all the dark countries and people among whom they are living. The glory of the apostolic age will return where the light of the pure Gospel has so long been extinguished. The missionary work will cease, and the efforts of American Christians will be crowned with a glorious consummation, and the blessings of my redeemed people will rest on your heads, and on the heads of our venerable missionaries. All soon pass away; but the names and memory of American Christians shall stand in Armenia—yea, in the heart of every Armenian—like a great monument, for generation after generation, till the end of this present dispensation.

By Pastor THOMAS BOYAJIAN,
Diarbekir, Turkey.

TO THE CHRISTIAN PUBLIC.

The unfortunate difficulties between the American Missionaries and the Armenian Protestant community of this capital have already become known to the public.

They originated in the attempt of the former to prevent the Rev. gentleman whom the Vlanga Church lately elected as their temporary pastor to preach in the chapel, and they were the first who gave publicity to these difficulties by their further attempt to keep him (the pastor) out of the chapel by civil power; and not being satisfied by this, they took upon themselves the responsibility to shut up forcibly, without any notice, the chapel at Yeni-Kapou, Vlanga, in which the congregation had worshipped for the last seventeen years, nailed up the schoolroom, and scattered the school children into the street, and gave into custody the Protestant Mukhdar, who was in the premises at the time, and represented to the authorities as burglars the officers of the Church who quietly unlocked the door and let the children into the schoolroom.

We notice with sorrow that our missionary friends are attempting to give a different colouring to this contest. They say it is a question of property with them. It has already been stated on the other side that the property issue is a false one forced by the missionaries upon a helpless people, on purpose to compel them, in obedience to their commands, to give up the pastor elect.

The Church never claimed the ownership of the chapel (although it asserts having contributed out of its poverty towards its purchase). They only contested the right of the missionaries so to control it as to drive the people out of it by violence. The missionaries claim that they are the proprietors of the religious work at Vlanga; the people deny that; they say, "We are by the grace of God and by your own admission the Church of the Lord Jesus Christ, and the work of evangelising our people is ours, and you are our helpers;" and really for several years past the work at Vlanga was carried on on this principle, that is, the Church there had the entire charge of supplying the pulpit.

With a desire to assist the public to form a correct idea—as far as possible—on the whole subject, we take the liberty to bring before the impartial public certain letters and papers written on this general subject, to which we also add the communications already published in the papers on both sides on same subject.

H. SIMON EUTUJIAN,

Pastor of Evangelical Armenian Church.

Constantinople, May 18, 1869.

OFFICIAL CIRCULAR.

The council of pastors and delegates which was convened at Vlanga on Friday, the 16th April, 1869, by the invitation of a portion of the Evangelical Armenian Church of that place, having examined the following points one by one and ascertained "that the Rev. Sdepan Eutujian was unanimously and in regular manner elected by the above-mentioned Church to be their temporary pastor, and therefore he is justly entitled to perform the pastoral duties over that Church and congregation," declare the same to the Churches of our Lord Jesus Christ throughout Turkey :—

First. In the month of December, 1868, Rev. Sdepan Eutujian was unanimously elected by the Church as their temporary pastor.

Second. The missionaries raising opposition to this election, difficulties arose concerning the support or salary of the pastor, consequently the formal invitation was delayed for about two months.

Third. During these two months nothing was said or done by the Church to reverse or recall their decision; on the contrary, every effort was made, both individually and collectively, to find a remedy for removing the above-mentioned financial difficulty.

Fourth. The committee of the Church having learned that there was a promise or a hope that a certain individual would assist the Church in this financial difficulty, called a Church meeting, and there stated this fact; the Church then, thinking the obstacle removed, by the vote of the majority, decided and arranged to put into execution what was decided on last December, that is to invite the Rev. Sdepan Eutujian to commence his services as pastor.

Fifth. The opposition or the assault against this arrangement was commenced on the part of the missionaries, and not from among the Church, and it was after much labour and many efforts that a minority was won over to the side of the missionaries, that is, they were induced to recall their vote.

Sixth. On the Sabbath day, February 21, after a public and

threatening declaration by the missionaries from the pulpit of the sanctuary that they were firmly resolved not to allow the choice of the Church to preach there, the Church, by the united voice of the majority, testified to and reconfirmed their former invitation to Rev. Sdepan Eutujian.

Seventh. Notwithstanding that so many threatening and unlawful efforts were made to compel the Church to recall their vote, the majority firmly adhere to their choice up to the present day.

Eighth. The entire worshipping congregation of Vlanga are unanimously with this portion of the Church, that is, they are in favour of Rev. Sdepan Eutujian's pastorate over their district.

Written by the choice and under the revision of the Council of Pastors and Delegates

> H. SIMON EUTUJIAN, Moderator.
> GARABED KAPRIELIAN, Clerk.
> ALEXANDER DJEDJIZIAN,
>   Pastor of Adapazar.
> ABRAHAM BOUGHDANIAN,
>   Pastor of Rodosto.
>
> Committee.

Constantinople, April 26, 1869.

To the Prudential Committee of the A. B. C. F. M., Boston, Mass., U. S. A.

CONSTANTINOPLE, April 19, 1869.

DEAR BRETHREN,—We, a council of pastors and delegates of the Evangelical Churches of Constantinople and its vicinity, having been invited by the Vlanga Church of this capital to inquire into the regularity of the call and invitation of Pastor Sdepan Eutujian to become their minister, have during this inquiry ascertained facts which have given us deep concern and sorrow; and we deem it our duty to yourselves and to the Churches we represent to lay them before you.

We have ascertained, beyond the shadow of a doubt, that at the invitation of your missionaries residing here to proceed to the choice of a temporary pastor, the Church worshipping in the Vlanga Chapel unanimously chose Pastor S. Eutujian, well known as the first pastor of the Church in Broosa, where he successfully laboured in the ministry for the space of twelve years, and as having already been acceptably employed by your society during the last twenty years. As soon, however, as your missionaries became acquainted with the fact of his election, they declared that they would withdraw their accustomed aid to the Church for the support of their pastor, and this, not on the ground of a doctrinal error or moral defect on his part, but, as they claimed, because he would not be a " useful pastor ;" by this expression we cannot understand that he would fail, in their opinion, to nourish and enlarge the Church, for his antecedents prove the contrary, and the man whom the missionaries desired the Church to elect has already broken up every Church of which he has had the charge long enough ; the only interpretation of which this language is capable, is that the missionaries believe that no pastor can be useful who fails to submit to any of their arbitrary requirements. The Church, however, succeeded in finding elsewhere the means to support their pastor. The missionaries then, forgetting the precept of the Master, that a house divided against itself cannot stand, sought to introduce dissensions and divisions into this hitherto harmonious Church, acting partly directly themselves, and partly through brethren, who, being in their pay, depend upon them for their living. They declared that whoever adhered to Pastor Sdepan would not be considered friendly to the missionaries, and threatened to eject them from Church membership, and in case of persecution or wrong, they will be left unprotected by the foreign embassies. Having by these means succeeded in withdrawing only a minority of the males or voting Church members, they applied to the civil authorities to prevent the entrance of the newly-elected pastor into the chapel, and even laid violent hands upon him to pull him out of the pulpit. Three of them subsequently went during the week to the chapel, forcibly ejected the school, the schoolmistress, and her family from the premises, even taking the sick out of their beds and carrying them out in their own arms; they then broke the locks, put on new ones instead, nailed up the schoolroom, and locked up the place ; they also delivered into the hands of the Turkish police a brother who was present in the chapel at the time.

The officers of the Church went and reopened both the school and the chapel. The missionaries, however, through the American Minister, complained to the Turkish Government that " their house had been forcibly opened and entered by unknown persons," but the Government authorities refused to recognise as a private house a building which had been dedicated and used as a house of worship for the last sixteen years ; they have acknowledged the right of the community who worship there and enjoy the ministrations of their chosen pastor. It is yet doubtful, however, whether your missionaries will not be able on legal grounds to deprive this people of a place of worship which was purchased for their special accommodation.

But we must call your special attention to another and a deeper wound inflicted by your missionaries upon this portion of the body of Christ. We have already stated that your missionaries had succeeded in inducing a certain number of the male Church members to withdraw their support of Pastor S. To these a few sisters had been added who depend upon the missionaries for their support. Not content with this, they gathered them into a private house, constituted them into a separate Church, and made them proceed to the choice of officers; they also appointed them a place of meeting in a private house, instead of the chapel. They declared several of the other brethren, among them some of the most experienced and of the longest standing, to be no Church members at all, and thus claim a majority on their own side. Those, however, who steadfastly adhere to their choice of Pastor S. are a majority, while nearly all the sisters and the entire congregation, as indeed all the Protestants of Constantinople, are on the same side.

Under these circumstances it is impossible for us, acting, as we must, as impartial judges in the case, and under our responsibility to our several Churches, and specially to the great Head of the Church, to do otherwise than stand by the imperilled right of our brethren and sisters of the Vlanga Church.

We have been brought up to respect and love your missionaries as the representatives of our sister Churches in America. But the despotic and unreasonable policy, introduced within a few years by young and inexperienced men, is fast breaking up the Churches of Christ already gathered in this land, and destroying the formerly high reputation and influence for good of these defenders of our faith. Should we be silent at such a moment, the blood of unnumbered souls would be required of us. Our appeals to your missionaries have not been heard. Shall we address ourselves in vain to you, whose larger experience enables you to take broader views and be influenced by more unselfish considerations?

In behalf of the Ecclesiastical Council now here convened, we remain your brethren in the fellowship of Christ,

H. SIMON EUTUJIAN, Moderator,
GARABED KAPRIELIAN, Clerk.

N.B.—The Armenian Evangelical Churches of Pera, Hasskeuy, Rodosto, Nicomidia, and Adapazar were represented in the Council by pastors and delegates, and the Churches of Diarbekir and Marash by pastors only.

To the Missionary Station at Constantinople.

BEBEK, March 4, 1869.

DEAR FRIENDS,—I have already, in friendly conversations, made known to you my dissent from the position you have recently taken in the affair of the Yeni-Kapou Church, and now I deem it proper, by your permission, to lay on your record the view I take of that position, as well as my reasons of dissent therefrom. To this end I beg leave to state—

First. The Yeni-Kapou Church was, organised years ago by the missionaries as an Evangelical Church, and to this day she is acknowledged as such, and is in regular Christian fellowship both with the missionaries and with her own sister Churches of the land.

Second. I believe the Yeni-Kapou Church is held by the missionaries and by her own sister Churches in repute of being as perfect as the other Evangelical Churches of the land are considered to be on an average, or at least nothing contrariwise is known to or said by either.

Third. The Yeni-Kapou Chapel is and has since its purchase, which was many years ago, been both publicly used and known as a Protestant meeting-house (though I believe it is the private property of the American Board entrusted to the care of its missionaries here, and that by legal right it can at pleasure be withdrawn from its present use), and in it the present Church was organised, and ever since its organisation had the continuous gratuitous use of it, and it was always intimated to them by the missionaries that in all probability they would continue to have that use, if not eventually have it presented to them as the gift of the American Board, as long as they would rightly remain in the Christian communion of the sister Evangelical Churches of the land.

Fourth. I firmly believe in the principle or love of liberty. It is held sacred both by the Church and State in all civilised lands, and for the proper development of the Churches under the missionary care, and for their becoming self-supporting, it is absolutely necessary that the missionaries, in their intercourse with these Churches, should respect that principle.

Fifth. I believe the withdrawal by the missionaries of the accustomed needed pecuniary aid from the Churches (as long as their being Christian and Evangelical Churches is not denied, and as long as they are in regular Christian fellowship both with the missionaries and with their sister Churches), is a dangerous interference with the freedom* of those Churches and a hindrance to their right Christian development.

Sixth. I understand that the missionaries, in taking their present position in the affair of the Church at Yeni-Kapou—not allowing them room in the chapel for *one* service on the Sabbath, to be conducted by their recently-chosen temporary pastor—they acted on the sole ground that said pastor, in their opinion, will not promote the good of the Church ; and although I believe that said opinion was and is held by them in honest conviction, yet I cannot resist, on equally honest conviction, considering their act under it as au unnecessary violation of the sacred principle of Church liberty, on the maintenance of which principle the permanent prosperity of the Churches so much depends, and I fear that if the precedent be persisted in, the state of things which has been unfortunately existing for a score of years between the missionaries and the Churches might not otherwise find a remedy.

With deep Christian sincerity and affection submitting the foregoing to your prayerful consideration, I subscribe myself,

Yours, &c.,

S. M. MINASIAN.

Mr. S. M. Minasian.

CONSTANTINOPLE, March 9, 1869.

MY DEAR SIR,—Your letter of the 4th instant to this station of our Mission was duly received, and I have been requested by my associates to reply to it.†

You speak of our " not allowing the Yeni-Kapou Church room in the chapel for one service on the Sabbath, to be conducted by their recently-chosen temporary pastor." It is astonishing that you could crowd so many mistakes into so few words. Any such request would have been entitled to a respectful consideration. But no such request has been refused, for the simple reason that no such request

---

* The missionaries trenched upon the liberties of the Church in refusing all aid to it, because it did not choose a pastor according to their prejudices or judgment, although they brought no charge of moral or doctrinal error against the pastor elect.

† Dr. Riggs, in this "reply," evades entirely the fourth and fifth topics of Mr. Minasian's letter, and it is left to the Christian public to judge of the fairness of the answer to the sixth.

has been made. Instead of a request of any sort we received a peremptory demand.* Instead of its being for one service, it was for the entire control of the pulpit. And instead of its being from the Church, it was from a minority of the Church, assembled at an unusual time, without public notice or any notice to some members.

Already a written protest against this whole proceeding has been signed by more members of the Church than were present at the meeting when the alleged call to Badveli Sdepan was made out. This protest with the signatures I have seen. Now when, in a full meeting,† called on purpose to ascertain the mind of the whole Church, and to which every member was specially invited, Badveli Sdepan, with that alleged "call" in his hand, interrupted the proceedings, utterly refused to have the protests (presented by members) considered, or to have the vote of eight members (for three of the eleven who voted for the "call," being members of other Churches, were not entitled to a vote) called in question in a full meeting of the Church, or to allow a vote to be taken as to who should preside (or any vote whatever), who is it who is "violating the sacred principle of Church liberty"—we, who tried to secure an expression of the Church's views, or Badveli Sdepan, who refused to allow that expression?

We desire, as you know, to see the true liberty of the Church understood and enjoyed. But do you not (with us) desire to have men understand the difference between rational liberty and that licence which would ignore the rights of others?

After duly considering the above facts I trust you will dismiss for ever from your mind the absurd idea of our attacking the liberty of the Y. K. Church.

In regard to the rules in accordance with which aid is granted to the Churches, they are the result of experience, and there is nothing in them which assails Church liberty, but their direct tendency is to develope it.

You are of course at liberty to show this note to Badveli Sdepan,

---

* The Church did not "peremptorily demand" the chapel; that was not then in question; it informed the missionaries that it would supply the pulpit and pay the pastor, supposing that, beyond all doubt, this was compliance with missionary principle often urged and set forth. See Mr. Herrick's letter on page 26.

† The missionaries had no right to get up a meeting of the Church against its pastor. No meeting of the Church could be had except called by the Church itself, and the meeting in which Pastor Sdepan opposed Mr. Herrick was itself an invasion of the Church's liberties.

towards whom I assure you we cherish no ill will, though we deeply regret the course he has taken.

I remain, on behalf of my associates and myself,

Most truly yours,

ELIAS RIGGS.

Rev. Dr. Riggs and Constantinople Station.

BEBEK, March 10, 1869.

DEAR FRIENDS,—Your favour of yesterday is before me, to which I beg leave to reply.

My expression of dissent from you in the affair of Yeni-Kapou Church, as it is very well known, was and is on matters that took place on February 19, 20, and 21 between the committee of that Church and the Constantinople Station, represented by Messrs. Herrick and Baldwin, and culminated in the peremptory refusal by the latter of an entrance to Pastor Sdepan (for preaching or otherwise) into the chapel; therefore anything that might have taken place subsequent to said dates I do not feel called upon either to defend or refute.

According to your own statement, I do not see that we differ as to facts. Our difference may be in the manner we state those facts. I say you did not allow the Church to have their own chosen man to conduct their service in a chapel, the use of which was granted them long ago, on the sole ground of your personal objection to said man as not being useful, and not that he was upheld only by a minority. That I state the case not erroneously I refer to the letter of Mr. Herrick to Pastor Sdepan, written on Feb. 20, as the very best evidence that can be desired upon this matter.* In the presence of that letter I cannot see how the correctness of my statement can be called into question. That letter speaks of "a committee of the Church informed us—that they have taken upon themselves the supply of the pulpit." The letter that is now before me speaks of "a peremptory demand for the entire control of the pulpit." I can see a little difference between these two statements, and like the form of the former better, as being probably more in accordance with the design of the committee that waited upon Mr. Herrick, as well as being nearer to the spirit of the privilege and usage accorded to Yeni-Kapou Church.

---

* See Mr. Herrick's letter on page 26.

In conclusion allow me to repeat what I mentioned elsewhere that if a majority of the Church is opposed to Pastor Sdepan's preaching to them in the chapel, let the decision be made in a regular way; then of course, everybody will respect their wish.

I remain, yours,

S. M. MINASIAN.

Rev. Dr. Riggs and Constantinople Station.

BEBEK, March 19, 1869.

DEAR FRIENDS,—In my previous correspondence with you, I have stated my opposition to your recent action in the affair of Yeni-Kapou Church, also my reasons for said opposition. My views briefly stated, amounted to these, viz.:—

First. That you hastily, and without sufficient reasons, withdrew the use of the Yeni-Kapou Chapel from the Church there, and have peremptorily refused an entrance into it to their temporary pastor.

Second. That your action under those circumstances was a dangerous interference with the liberty of the Church, and it would eventually, if not corrected, prevent their development. I have entered into the correspondence with you on this subject after a long consideration, and with anxious and prayerful desire to induce you to recede from a wrong or questionable position; but I do now fear that the design or spirit which impelled me to act in this matter was not understood, or rather it was misunderstood. Therefore, I feel it a solemn duty to myself, and to the Evangelical cause in this land, to ask you to allow me to forward the copies of our correspondence, together with some other papers, between the Church, yourselves, and Pastor Sdepan—bearing on this subject—to the Prudential Committee at Boston, also to lay the same papers before the enlightened Christian public.

I remain, most truly yours,

S. M. MINASIAN.

Constantinople Station.

BEBEK, March 23, 1869.

DEAR FRIENDS,—I must apologise for writing so soon after forwarding you mine of the 19th inst., but as I expressed then, I fear that my object in taking action in reference to the present unhappy affairs might be misunderstood. My aim in this matter is, of course, not to prove that your course is wrong, and that you are erring in judgment, or that I have an infallible judgment and have the highest motive for thus acting in the affair, &c., &c., neither I do believe you look upon those personal questions as the chief points in the case. The real question in the controversy is, what course will promote the highest good of the Churches, or, in other words, will lay the Evangelical religion on firm bases in the land. As an answer to this question on my part, I beg leave to quote here a portion of a private letter I wrote to Dr. Riggs on the 1st inst.: " I think I have already said to other friends that *it is and has ever been* my deep conviction that the only way to promote the cause of Evangelical religion in this land will be found in cordial and Christian and wisely planned co-operation between the missionary body and the Evangelical Churches of the land ; and I feel that I have so much more reason to mourn over the fact that that Christian co-operation and confidence never existed in a satisfactory degree, and that it never existed in so little degree, if I am not mistaken, as at present, while friends who know me will admit that for the last seventeen years, in all my honest endeavours for the good of this land, I always, and by the use of all the means at my command, aimed for the creation or increase of that most desired harmony and Christian confidence between the parties mentioned." In conclusion, dear brethren, allow me to say in earnest that God will never bless the work in this land unless the Churches and the missionaries labour in harmony.

Yours,

S. M. MINASIAN.

The following is the only answer the Rev. missionaries made to the preceding three letters of Mr. Minasian, in which not the slightest notice is taken of the grave charges made against them, as though they were matters of no account :—

Mr. S. M. Minasian.

CONSTANTINOPLE, March 26, 1869.

MY DEAR SIR,—We have not had a meeting of the Station since receiving your note of the 19th until to-day. I am directed to reply to it that we offer no objection to your communicating to the Prudential Committee all that has passed between us on the subject of the Yeni-Kapou Church. In reference to securing an early answer from them, you would save time by giving us a copy of what you send. Otherwise their first step would naturally be to send us a copy, and ask for what we have to say in reference to it.

As to publishing these communications, or anything on the subject, we do not see what good can be gained by it. You must decide this point according to your own judgment. In our view, Christians should be slow to throw before the world their differences, at least until every effort has been exhausted to reconcile them.

I remain, on behalf of the Station, yours truly,

ELIAS RIGGS.

Rev. Dr. Riggs and Constantinople Station.

BEBEK, March 29, 1869.

DEAR FRIENDS,—In answer to my note of the 19th instant, I received yours of the 26th instant, announcing that you have no objection to my communicating to the Prudential Committee all that has passed between us on the subject of the Yeni-Kapou Church, and suggest that, in order to secure an early answer from them, I might give you a copy of what I may send. I will endeavour to comply with your suggestion, unless, in view of my leaving for U. S. so soon, I might deem it desirable to present the case to the Prudential Committee personally; in that event, I will not be prepared to furnish you beforehand with the copy of the communication. In reference to bringing our differences before the Christian public opinion, you say, "Christians should be slow to throw before the world their differences, at least until every effort has been exhausted to reconcile them." My own views are quite in accordance with that statement, and I think the same rule also applies to the bringing of our differences before the Prudential Committee; but you forget that by ignoring my letters, written to you expressly on those differences, you deprived me altogether of the means of reconciliation, and thus the responsibility of whatever I may deem it proper to do rests entirely with you. You deny a hearing to this cause; you either don't regard the cause as worth your attention, or may be myself and these poor Churches. We thought almost any case respectfully represented deserved a respectful answer. We must have a hearing at some tribunal—the Prudential Committee, or the Christian public, or both. In this connexion it may not be improper for me to remind you that the life or death of the Evangelical Churches of this land depend on the principle involved in our present controversy.

You lay solemn responsibilities upon the Churches, but when they exercise their will in the discharge of those responsibilities, you trample that will under foot. Under those circumstances, it is absurd to say that you are trying to make them independent and self-supporting Churches; your course, instead of doing that, is calculated to destroy whatever particle of life and independence they may possess. I know you say we don't touch their independence. If they have their own church, their own school-house, built by their own money, and if they support their pastor and their schools, then let them choose any one they like. This seems like mocking poverty. In that case, would they ask you? What power would you have? Would not your saying " We give you leave," be ridiculous? Would not your prohibition be equally so? The Churches must have liberty to do what they think is right. Liberty to do your will is strange liberty. That you act under the highest motives does not change the wrong principle into a right one, neither do I believe God blesses a wrong act because it is intended for good. Your difficulties with these Churches are not of recent origin, they are of twenty years' standing, and I very much fear that the same unreasonable course of laying responsibilities upon, but withholding the corresponding freedom of action from them, may have had much to do in creating and in keeping alive those difficulties. I know in this controversy I labour under disadvantage, because it so happens that the cause I advocate is that of feeble and imperfect Churches, yet I need not be ashamed of that, because it is not the first time that people of that class stood in need of sympathy.

I remain, most truly yours,

S. M. MINASIAN.

On the 31st of March Rev. Dr. Riggs, acknowledging the receipt of this letter on his own part, "as an individual," says, " Yours of yesterday has been received, and will, of course, be communicated to my associates. I do not see anything in it which requires an answer from them."

Rev. Sdepan Eutujian.

CONSTANTINOPLE, Feb. 20, 1869.

DEAR SIR,—A committee of the Vlanga Church informed us last evening that they have taken upon themselves the supply of the pulpit, commencing with to-morrow, and have invited you to preach in our chapel. In view of our recent action in reference to your preaching here, this action of the Church is surprising and much to be regretted. Of course, a Church has the right to select its own minister, when it pays his salary* and all other expenses, and holds its worship in a building of its own. The Vlanga Chapel is the property of the Board, and in our charge, and no man has the right to preach there without our consent. We do not consent to your preaching there. I said this to the committee that called upon me yesterday, and requested them to recall their invitation to you. They replied that there was not time to assemble the Church. Therefore I write you this note that there may be no misunderstanding. We shall ourselves preach there to-morrow, D.V.; so I trust you will not come down.

In behalf of the Missionaries, yours truly,

GEO. F. HERRICK.

---

* We claim that feeble Churches have liberties, and not only strong Churches, which have no occasion to ask anything of anybody; we have ascertained by careful inquiries that the feeble Churches in America are allowed to choose their own pastors before they are able to support them entirely. All we ask is the same right for our Churches here.

FROM THE "LEVANT TIMES AND SHIPPING GAZETTE."

THE PROTESTANT MEETING-HOUSE, STAMBOUL.

To the Editor of the " Levant Times and Shipping Gazette."

SIR,—Some time since a question arose between the American missionaries and the congregation of the Protestant Church at Stamboul, as to whether, in view of the former paying the largest part of the salary of the pastor over that Church, the latter, after making a choice of a person to fill that office temporarily, should give up their choice because the missionaries objected to him on the ground (not of moral or religious character) of usefulness, and advised them to give him up. On the congregation deciding that they would rather forego the aid than give up their choice, the missionaries took upon them-selves the responsibility of forcibly shutting up the Protestant Meeting-house of Stamboul on last Tuesday, the 6th inst., turned the children out of the schoolroom into the street, and also gave in custody a Protestant who happened to be in the chapel at the time of this violent action.

We regret very much to see the missionaries enter into such a con-test, because, whatever its merits in other respects may be, it is an outrageously unequal one. It is between the humble, poor, and unlearned on one side, and the influential and learned on the other ; and we fear that its effect might be that the missionaries may lose their influence for good on a class of people over whom we desire to exert Christian influence, and for whom we have all been long and arduously labouring to induce them to receive our Evangelical faith.

ONE OF THE PEOPLE.

Constantinople, April 10, 1869.

To the Editor of the " Levant Times and Shipping Gazette."

SIR,—In answer to the statements concerning the Protestant Meeting-house in Stamboul, made by " One of the People " in your issue of yesterday, I beg leave to say—

First. The house is the sole property of the American Mission. They bought it, paid for it, and hold a clear title to it. Their ownership has been frequently acknowledged by the Church and congregation, who have been permitted to worship there free of charge.

Second. Some time since a discontented minority of the local Church attempted to take the control of the pulpit out of our hands, and to place it in the hands of a native preacher violently opposed to us. As the result of conferences we were assured by the head of the Protestant Armenian Community that the said preacher would not occupy our pulpit without our consent. But when the violent faction saw that a clear majority of the local Church was against them, they determined to do by force what they could not do in an orderly way. Accordingly, a week ago last Sabbath, before we could reach it, the pulpit was occupied by said native preacher, with whom came a large number of outsiders to protect him in his seizure of the pulpit. We, of course, demanded the pulpit, and when it was refused, retired. To prevent the recurrence of such a scene we went to the building on Tuesday, requested the teacher (who also occupies our premises rent free, as does the school) to remove her effects and the school to another part of the same premises (separated from the chapel part by iron doors), where there were good empty rooms at her disposal, also rent free. The removal effected, we closed the chapel part of our premises, intending to open them as usual on Sunday. We used no violence to any one. On the afternoon of the same day certain individuals broke into the building, and seized a house belonging exclusively to us, and to the control of which they have no right whatsoever. The contest is between a perfectly clear title and no title at all, between undoubted owners and a body of usurpers, who claim that because we have allowed them to worship there free of rent, they have acquired the right to break into our property forcibly and hold it against us.

ONE OF THE AMERICAN MISSIONARIES.

Constantinople, April 13, 1869.

To the Editor of the "Levant Times and Shipping Gazette."

Sir,—Letters having been published respecting the difficulties which have arisen between the American missionaries and the native Protestant Church and community in Constantinople, your readers will perhaps be interested to know something of Pastor Sdepan Eutujian—the "man" whom the missionaries refused to acknowledge as pastor of the above-mentioned community in spite of its unanimous choice. He is one of the oldest Protestant native pastors, a man known in all the country as a defender of the truths of our religion. The subjoined testimony, of undoubted authority, will suffice to introduce him to the public.

I am, &c.,

AN ARMENIAN PROTESTANT.

Constantinople, April 14.

(Copy.)

The undersigned, in behalf of the Missionary Station of the American Board at Constantinople, certifies that the Rev. Sdepan Eutujian was educated in the Seminary of the American Board at Bebek, where he pursued with fidelity and success the scientific and theological course, and, believing him in accordance with his own profession to be called of God to preach the Gospel, the Station assisted in his licensure and ordination as pastor of the Broosa Church, and has always been gratified with his faithful labours and Christian life and sound doctrine among the people of his charge, so far as known to them during his pastorate of twelve years unto this day.

By order of the Constantinople Station,

(Signed) C. HAMLIN.

P.S.—In the month of July following Pastor Sdepan was chosen by a majority of the representatives to the office of Askabed* of the nation, in regard to which election the missionaries of the American Board and of other societies in Constantinople, having been invited to express their opinion, it was unanimously approved, and a committee was appointed to aid in its execution. But difficulties having arisen from the opposition of the first Askabed's party, Pastor Sdepan, not wishing to be the occasion of further divisions, sent in his declinature and voluntarily withdrew.

(Signed) C. HAMLIN.

April 2, 1863.

To the Editor of the "Levant Times and Shipping Gazette."

Sir,—In your issue of April 14 "One of the American Missionaries" attempts to make an answer to the letter of "One of the

* Civil head of the community.

People " about the scandalous affair in the district of Vlanga. I beg leave to answer him as follows :—

1. " The house is" not "the sole property of the American Mission." Not one of the men who are now endeavouring to get possession of it ever paid a para towards it. The money was given partly by the Protestant community of Constantinople, and at their request partly by benevolent individuals in America. All these parties gave the money for the specific purpose of furnishing the Protestants of the capital with a house of worship, and not to give the American missionaries a house which they can sell or use as they like.

2. Your correspondent endeavours to draw away the attention from the real point at issue, which is this : This place of worship has been used by common consent by the Church and congregation living in the quarter of Vlanga, for whose benefit it was purchased. It is the custom both of native and American Protestant Churches, and their fully recognised right, to choose their own pastor or preacher. In accordance with this right the missionaries of the capital invited the Vlanga Church at the beginning of the year to choose a pastor, with the promise of paying themselves three-quarters of his salary. In accordance the Church unanimously elected Pastor Sdepan Eutujian—a man of whose character you can judge from the certificate published in your paper of April 15, and who has already been honourably employed by these and other American missionaries for the last twenty years. The missionaries have repeatedly and publicly promised not to interfere with the choice of a pastor unless he be unsound in doctrine and morals. But in the present case they desired to put into that important post a creature of their own, whom they could use to accomplish their own purposes. They therefore declared that they could not pay anything towards the salary of the said pastor, and when the Church informed them that they had themselves found the means to provide for it, they declared they would prevent his preaching in the chapel, and even threatened to push him out of the pulpit by the hand of the police.

Seeing that these means failed of accomplishing their object, the missionaries then endeavoured to divide the hitherto unanimous Church ; they declared that whoever wanted Pastor S. E. was the personal enemy of the mission, and " would be by them excommunicated, and in case of difficulty would be left unprotected by the foreign embassies." Failing in this way also to obtain a majority on their side, they declared their intention to examine the right of every one to Church membership, in order to eject those who did not suit them. Again they failed, for the people loudly called for a religious commission to examine and decide the point in litigation, which the missionaries refused.

Finally, when everything else had failed, the Rev. triumvirate went in haste to the chapel, accompanied by locksmiths, forcibly took off the lock of the door, and drove out the people who were within— not, as they claim, gently persuaded them to remove, for they took up the sick with their own hands, and the school children were turned into the street; they then made fast the doors, after violently ejecting persons who came to entreat them to desist, and even delivered one of them into the hands of the police. The doors were opened again, the school children, schoolmistress, &c., were taken back to their places, but it was done lawfully and regularly by the constituted authorities.

You can judge, Sir, by the preceding account, of which every word can be proved true before a court of justice, how much credit is to be given to the statements of "One of the American Missionaries." The contest, as you see, is not "between a clear title and no title at all," but between a people who claim the right to choose their own pastor, and men who require unconditional submission.

I am, &c.,

ONE OF THE PEOPLE.

Constantinople, April 15, 1869.

To the Editor of the " Levant Times and Shipping Gazette."

Sir,—The second letter of " One of the People," in your issue of Saturday, is full of misrepresentations; but we must decline to enter into a newspaper controversy with the author. If any of your readers has the least desire to see the evidence of the truth of my previous statement, that the building in question is the sole property of the American Mission, we shall be happy to show them, at our depôt in Stamboul, a document legalised at the American Consulate at the time of the purchase, in which it is expressly stated that the purchase was made " entirely and exclusively with the money of the American Board of Commissioners for Foreign Missions."

I am, &c.,

ONE OF THE AMERICAN MISSIONARIES.

Constantinople, April 19, 1869.

FROM THE "LEVANT HERALD."

The following, in reply to some statements of the *Manzoumeï Efkiar*, appears in the *Avedaper*, an Armeno-Turkish paper published by the American Missionaries :—

Inaccurate statements having been published in certain papers of this city, concerning recent events relating to the Yeni-Kapou Protestant place of worship, we give the following brief account of the matter : The Protestant place of worship and school is in a house bought and held by the American missionaries as trustees for the American Board of Missions. The missionaries have granted the use of portions of this building, rent free, to the local Protestant community, for purposes of school and chapel, themselves paying nearly all expenses of teacher and preacher, from the first till now, and often preaching, and always worshipping with the native community themselves. One of this number has sometimes resided in the building. Their ownership and right of control have been repeatedly acknowledged by the community. Eight weeks ago, a small irregular meeting of the local Church abruptly and indecorously demanded to put into the pulpit as preacher a man whom they knew to be unacceptable to the missionaries, and were warned, as was this preacher himself, and the civil head of the Protestant community also, that his attempting to preach there would be regarded as a trespass, and they were assured officially that he would not preach against their permission in their chapel. But when the party supporting this preacher saw that a clear majority of the Church had pronounced against them, and for co-operation with the missionaries, they became desperate, and, in violation of promise, and directly against the consent of the missionaries, put the above-mentioned preacher into the pulpit on Sabbath morning, the 4th inst. The following Tuesday, the missionaries went to the house, gave notice to the teacher of the school that she must immediately remove the school into an unoccupied room in the wooden part of the house, and remove her own room there also. The empty part of the building, within the stone walls, was securely closed and locked. The statements that violence was used are utterly false. The missionaries designed to open the place as usual for public worship on the Sabbath, and they left those occupying the other portion of their property (the wooden house), with the school, undisturbed for the present. But toward evening of the same day the lock was broken in, and the premises forcibly seized and held by certain lawless persons. Complaint of this violation of their property was of course made to the authorities by the missionaries. Upon this, persons were sent to Yeni-Kapou to make inquiries into the facts of the case, and the head of the Protestant community was asked for information concerning the affair. Having done thus much without coming to any decision in regard to the merits of the case, official action was deferred for one week, in the hope of some mutually satisfactory arrangement being made. The statement that the missionaries cited a priest and the leading members of the community before the police is utterly false.

To the Editor of the " Levant Herald."

Sir,—In your issue of April 14 is an account, professedly taken from the Armenian paper published by the American missionaries of this city, which contains so many erroneous statements that, although the undersigned belongs to neither party, he deems it but fair to correct them. The chapel at Yani-Kapou used to be a private house, but has been dedicated and used as a church for the last sixteen years. It was bought at the earnest request of the congregation, who have there been accommodated, and a firman was on the point of being issued recognising it as such. The missionaries would never have thought of claiming the ownership in it for their society, much less of shutting it up, which it is well known is contrary to the wishes of the said society, were it not for the purpose of compelling the native Church to give up their undoubted right to choose their own minister. The article from the *Avedaper* makes a simply false statement when it says that "a clear majority" were opposed to the pastor. I have myself seen the documents which prove that his choice was unanimous. Strange to say, the Sultan's rayahs have given a noble example of moderation and forbearance to the foreign teachers who have come to enlighten their "darkened minds." It was the missionaries who sent for police to take their quiet opponents into custody, who surrounded the pulpit to prevent the people's choice from entering it, who *broke* the locks of the building, who compelled those who occupy it to vacate the premises, who took the sick in their own arms out of their beds, and turned out the school into the street, although they claim that they merely removed them to another part of the house. This is really a distinct house, though it communicates by an iron door, and it is but mockery to say that any addition could be made to its already crowded tenants. This letter would be too long were I to endeavour to point out all the erroneous statements to which I refer.

Suffice it to say that, if the " American Mission " has obtained a foot-
ing in Turkey, it was done by the labours of love of a generation now
gone ; but the despotism of their present successors is fast destroying
the works of the " fathers."

I am, &c.,

Constantinople, April 16.   FAIR PLAY.

To the Editor of the " Levant Herald."

Sir,—Letters have been published in your and other papers on the
part of the American missionaries respecting the differences between
them and the Protestant congregation at Vlanga in Constantinople.
In these letters the whole question has been made to turn upon the
legal ownership, and a claimed consequent right of control, of the
Church building and premises. This is a false issue. The true point
at issue is whether the Churches should be so independent that they
can choose their own pastors and enjoy their ministrations undisturbed.
The following letter refers to a proposition which was about to be
made by a gentleman, himself a native, who has no connection with
the American mission, to assume the payment of all the money now
disbursed by them, for the purpose of removing all cause of litigation.
The missionaries were aware that this highly promising plan was
about to be presented to them, and the unfortunate contest at Vlanga
about the Church building was conjured up by them in order to
prevent its realisation.

I am, &c.,

Constantinople, April 20.   AN INDEPENDENT.

To —— , Esq.

My Dear Sir,—You ask me to state to you the impressions which
I received in the conversations we had as to the possibility of restor-
ing harmony to the Evangelical work in Constantinople. Our first conversations were in regard to Haskeui, for which we had a plan that
seemed to promise good, but which proved abortive. Next, you proposed, as a matter of consultation, the plan of seeing how much the
Churches and congregations here could be induced to raise for the
support of all their religious institutions, you engaging to supply the
deficiency to the amount of three or four hundred pounds a-year,
thus relieving the mission and station from all financial connection
with the churches. You expressed the hope and the earnest desire
that in this way a truly harmonious co-operation between the mis-

sionaries and the Churches would spring up and the work be rescued from ruin. I fully agreed with your views, and thought the station would hail the proposition with joy, and that it afforded an opportunity to take a *new start*. I supposed also that all would regard your having so prominent a part in it, and being willing to contribute so generously towards it, as a pledge that the movement would be such as all might co-operate with who labour and pray for the establishment of the kingdom of Christ in this land. You expressed the conviction that with freedom of action and consequent entire responsibility on the part of these feeble Churches a new spirit would come in and efface the many unpleasant feelings which exist. I fully agreed with you in this view, and felt strongly desirous that it should be tried on the basis you proposed—freedom and responsibility. If it should work badly it could hardly be worse than the present. I will not enter into events which followed, but I do sincerely regret that the experiment was not made.

Yours truly,

C. HAMLIN.

P.S.—I mentioned your proposal to Mr. Bliss, and he seemed to think favourably of it. He remarked to this effect, that the project would need to be stated in full, and each part have its duties and responsibilities defined. We were on board the steamer, and the conversation was not continued.

Bebek, March 22, 1869.   C. H.

To the Editor of the "Levant Herald."

SIR,—Your correspondent "Fair Play" having expressed the opinion that the present generation of American missionaries in Turkey are pursuing a course of action towards the native Churches quite unlike that of their predecessors, we, the undersigned, having been connected with the mission more than a quarter of a century, feel called upon to say over our own signatures that the principles which guide the present missionaries are precisely those which guided the "fathers." They have always claimed and exercised control over the building in question; they always claimed and exercised the right to give or withhold aid to the native Churches or communities, according as, in the exercise of their own judgment, giving or withholding would promote the prosperity of the work for which they were sent to this country. They and their successors in this respect only obey the instructions of the Society which has sent them forth, and are responsible to it alone for the exercise of their judgment. At the same time, the "fathers" and those who are now in this field, while they can never surrender the right of control of property belonging to their Society, and of the funds entrusted to them by that Society, have ever desired to exercise this right in the kindest spirit towards the native Churches. In the present case, when the missionaries were asked several months since to aid the Vlanga Church in the support of a preacher whom the Church had chosen, they declined to do so, and assigned their reasons in writing. If " Fair Play " has seen any document referring to the choice of a preacher, it undoubtedly refers to this action several months ago, whereas the assertions of the missionaries respect subsequent votes of the Church cancelling that action ; it is upon these subsequent votes that the missionaries found the declaration that a clear majority is on the side upon which they have affirmed it to be. " Fair Play " should have examined all the documents, and heard both sides, before presuming to pronounce judgment. A written protest against the pretended unanimous choice has been signed by a majority of the members of the Church question. We 'aver that the principal statements of " Fair Play's " article are false, and we think the candid reader will judge so from a simple comparison of them with those of the article quoted from the *Avedaper.*

We are, &c.,

ELIAS RIGGS.
EDWIN E. BLISS.

Constantinople, April 20.

To the Editor of the " Levant Herald."

Sir,—The American missionaries, the Rev. Messrs. Riggs and Bliss, have in your issue of April 21 found fault with the impartial statements I had made respecting the unfortunate affair at Vlanga. It had been reported that they had disapproved the rashness of the triumvirate who were the principal actors of the said scandalous affair; they now father their doings, and thus render hopeless the prospect of amendment. There are two points in their letter to which I reply as follows :—

1. Messrs. Riggs and Bliss claim to belong to the former generation of missionaries, and that the policy of the mission has not changed. This is a heavy charge to bring against such men as the "fathers,"

Goodell, Temple, and Dwight, against Benjamin and Everett, and some yet living and honoured among us, Hamlin and Schauffler. When they can prove that any or all of these men have attempted to pull out of the pulpit, by force, preachers of the Gospel against whose doctrine or morals there was not the shadow of a charge; that they have violently shut up churches, scattered schools, and taken away the sick by force from their beds; that they have annulled or protested against the united and moderate advice of a council of the pastors and delegates of the Churches, sought to disrupt Churches and form new ones on the simple authority of their own wills, and have not even spared those of their own number who have failed to approve their strange innovations, but have brought about their excision from their body without trial or regular judgment; whenever they can show, I say, that the "fathers" have also done these and similar things, then shall we acknowledge that the "policy" of the mission has not changed; but until then, we shall rightly maintain that Messrs. Riggs and Bliss belong to the later generation of American missionaries, whose "unavoidable destiny" is to destroy the work of the "fathers."

2. Messrs. Riggs and Bliss consider that the choice of Pastor Sdepan Eutujian by the Church was unanimous, but claim that the majority are now against him; they advance in proof a document. But what says the document? Not that the undersigned deem the pastor unfit for his office, but that, the missionaries being opposed to him, they desire to give him up for the sake of peace. And it was a minority,* not a majority, of the Church that signed the document, as found and solemnly declared by the council of pastors and delegates from the surrounding Churches, which has just sat and passed judgment in the case.

I am, Sir, yours, &c.,

Constantinople, April 23, 1869. FAIR PLAY.

To the Editor of the "Levant Herald."

SIR,—Neither the "fathers" nor any of the present generation of American missionaries in Turkey have done one of the things charged in the communication signed "Fair Play," and published in the *Herald* of yesterday.

We are, Sir, &c.,

ELIAS RIGGS,

Constantinople, April 26. EDWIN E. BLISS.

---

* See page 15.

To the Editor of the " Levant Herald."

SIR,—Your anonymous correspondent " Fair Play" has had the hardihood to use my name in the interests of the foul cause* which he advocates. I wish all concerned to understand that I consider the use of my name in this connexion slanderous, and that of the missionaries of sainted memory sacrilegious.

Bebek, April 28. W. G. SCHAUFFLER.

To the Editor of the " Levant Herald."

SIR,—Though I do not pretend to be responsible for any one's statements, yet justice impels me to say that I am prepared to prove by unimpeachable testimony most of the charges brought forward in your and other papers against the missionaries by " Fair Play " and others, in behalf of the outraged Armenian Protestant community, notwithstanding the denial of the same by Messrs. Riggs, Bliss, and others.

I am, &c.,

Bebek, April 28. S. M. MINASIAN.

CIRCULAR

Respectfully submitted to the members of the Mission of the American Board at Constantinople, and of the Evangelical Armenian Congregation of Yeni-Kapou.

Whereas difficulties have arisen between the missionaries of the A. B. C. F. M. and the Evangelical Armenian congregation at Yeni-Kapou, for the settlement of which application has been made to the Turkish authorities ; and whereas we are warned of the unseemliness of brother going to law with brother, and that before the unbelievers, and feel convinced that an effort ought to be made to heal those differences by a free and brotherly conference between both parties, with earnest prayer for the Divine blessing, the undersigned, therefore, beg respectfully to request the missionaries of the Board and the

---

(*) Our venerable friend Dr. Schauffler, through some influence, has been misled to take the universally recognised "irrepressible conflict" between the weak and the strong, in the present case, for a "foul cause." We submit to the unbiassed judgment of the Christian public whether less "hardihood" is evinced in calling the friendly allusion of "Fair Play" to his and other honoured names "slanderous" and "sacrilegious."

committee of the said congregation, or such parties as have been acting with and for them, to meet at the Bible Magazine on Monday, the 26th inst., at half-past 2 P.M., to consider the following basis of agreement—viz. :—

First. As the Vlanga Chapel was purchased by funds mainly contributed by friends in America, the Protestant community consents not to contest the right of the missionaries to control the same, provided they will not undertake to shut it up against the worshippers as long as the Church maintains Orthodox Evangelical doctrines.

Second. That the missionaries shall agree to grant to Vlanga congregation the use of the schoolroom during the week and of the chapel for half the day on the Sabbath, with access to the premises on other occasions as in time past.

Third. That the missionaries acknowledge the right of the Church to choose its pastor or preacher; but in case the Vlanga Church, in exercise of this right, shall choose as their pastor or preacher one against whom the missionaries formally protest on doctrinal and moral ground, and lodge with the clerk of the congregation within three days after they have received official intimation of the said election by the congregation, the Church agree that such person shall not officiate in either capacity until the choice be approved by a suitable council of the sister Churches regularly called for that purpose, it being understood that such right of protest is allowed to the mission only so long as they continue to aid the congregation in the support of their pastor or preacher.

Fourth. That in consideration of existing circumstances the congregation at Vlanga agree to consider all their action, as to the choice of Rev. Sdepan Eutujian as their pastor, to be null and void, and to proceed to a new election at an interval of three months from the date of agreement, it being understood that during that interval only those will officiate in the chapel who have not taken any part in the late contest.

Bebek, April 24, 1869.   S. M. MINASIAN.

Mr. S. M. Minasian.

STAMBOUL, April 26, 1869.

DEAR SIR,—The missionaries instruct me to inform you that they cannot consent to attend a meeting for the consideration of the proposals of your circular of April 24.

I am, truly yours,

H. A. SCHAUFFLER.

Rev. Dr. Clark, Secretary of American Board and Mission House, Boston, Mass., U.S.A.

VIENNA, May 24, 1869.

MY DEAR SIR,—I sent you a telegram from Pesth on the 20th inst., requesting you to suspend the action of the missionaries at Constantinople against the Protestant community until you would hear the case. I have no time to tell you now what the "case" is, but presume you know all about it by the reports of the missionaries. My only wish is, that the missionaries might be advised to refer such an important question to the Prudential Committee before or instead of appealing to the Turkish Court, as they did. I enclose the copy of the note I addressed to Constantinople station to-day on the same subject.

With kindest regards I subscribe myself, yours,

S. M. MINASIAN,

Rev. Dr. Riggs, Constantinople Station.

VIENNA, May 24, 1869.

MY DEAR FRIEND,—I sent a telegram on the 20th inst., from Pesth, to the Prudential Committee at Boston, as my telegram on the same day to you informed you, that they might suspend your proceedings in court against the Protestant community until they will hear the case. I do not know whether my message will be intelligible to them or not, nor whether they will think it advisable to interfere in the present stage of the case; still I thought the idea was a good one to refer the case to the Prudential Committee and wait for their decision, rather than to appeal to the Turkish Courts, and I feel very sorry that the thought did not occur to me while I was in Constantinople, so that I might have suggested it to both parties.

It was very much to be regretted that nothing was done by the station in the way to effect the settlement of the difficulty without going before the courts. I write in haste. With kindest regards to all the brethren now in Constantinople, and with an earnest prayer that the Divine blessing may attend them in all their deliberations, I remain, most sincerely yours,

S. M. MINASIAN.

S. M. Minasian, Esq., Constantinople.

MISSIONARY HOUSE, BOSTON, U.S.A., May 31, 1869.

MY DEAR SIR,—Your telegram of May 20 was received the same day, and a week after came a paper giving the action of an *ex-parte* council in regard to the difficulties in the Vlanga Church. No action has yet been taken in the case by the Prudential Committee of the American Board. Amid so many conflicting statements it is not easy to arrive at the truth, and it seems better to wait till all the facts shall have been laid before us, and till the passions excited by this most unhappy difference shall have had time to cool, and the true Christain sentiment that we believe to exist shall have made itself felt.

It is hardly necessary for me to express my surprise and profound regret that any such difference and misunderstanding should have arisen among Christian brethren sincerely devoted to one common cause, and that it should have become a matter of such public notoriety and scandal to the Christian name. The injury done to the cause of Christ in Constantinople, and elsewhere in the Turkish empire, and wherever the press has carried the painful tidings, is immense, and very grave responsibilities rest on every man who by inconsiderate haste, ill-temper, or unchristian spirit, has fostered or given publicity to an evil which, as a raging fire, every true friend of the Gospel should have tried to put down as soon as possible.

We cannot but believe that if time had been taken for kindly counsel, and a full and free conference upon all questions in dispute, in a spirit of Christian love and forbearance, all difficulties could have been adjusted. It is far better to suffer wrong for a time, if need be, than to stir up evil passions by hasty and violent action; especially when this wrong is suffered from the hands of those who, when better informed, will be only too glad to make proper amends.

The great respect and high personal regard entertained toward you by our committee generally, and particularly by those who have had the pleasure of your personal acquaintance, make them regret all the more that any difference of sentiment should exist between you and our missionaries; and we cannot but hope that a better understanding of each other's views will have been gained ere this reaches you, and entire good feeling restored.

As you are well aware, neither we nor our missionaries have any personal ends to gain by the efforts we are making for the spiritual welfare of the Armenians in Turkey. The love of Christ alone constrains us to make the large expenditure of money and of missionaries for this object. The Armenian Missions have had a large share of the funds placed at our disposal for the promotion of the missionary enterprise. We have spent the more freely in the hope that the Armenian Protestants would soon be able to carry forward the great work of evangelization in the Turkish Empire without assistance from abroad. This hope is greatly encouraged by the spirit of self-denial and earnest devotion to the cause of Christ, and hearty co-operation with the missionaries, evinced by many of the Churches, making them bright and shining examples to the Christian world.

Considering our motives and object, the self-denial and sacrifices made by the Christian men and women who have left home and country, and positions of honour, ease, and influence, to go abroad—circumstances which you can fully understand and appreciate from your acquaintance with this country—is it too much to ask for a kindly forbearance, for a generous Christian consideration for particular acts of ours or of our missionaries that may not at once commend themselves to your judgment, but which may be modified or recalled upon a better understanding of all the facts in the case?

We do not suppose that we ourselves, nor our missionaries, nor our brethren in the Armenian Churches, are exempt from the possibility of mistakes on practical questions of duty or expediency. But I would hope that the spirit of Christ in all who bear His name, of whatever nationality, will be a spirit of love, of forbearance, and of Christian charity.

It has seemed to me that our Armenian brethren in Constantinople and vicinity have not always appreciated aright the one supreme object of our missionary labours—not to attempt to import the Christian civilization of this country, the fruit of many years of culture and discipline, all ready made as it were, but to lay the basis of an equally noble civilization, not American, but Armenian. The foundation of our culture and prosperity as a people is the Gospel of Christ, with its quickening energy and inspiring motives, prompting believers to seek for themselves and their families the best culture and the enjoyment of all the arts and blessings of civilized life. Mere education, however complete and wide in its range, cannot secure this. The civilization of Paris and Berlin and Vienna is not of the English and American type. It is not such as we would introduce or help to develop in our mission fields. Men are everywhere eager to reap the fruits, before they have time to grow and to ripen on the soil. They crave the forms and the accomplishments of cultured life before they get the substance, and so we are urged to set up fashionable schools, and to introduce modes of living entirely out of keeping with the real wants of the people, as well as their best interests. Men of great learning and piety among our fathers cherished simple habits of life, and lived in humble dwellings that their children would now despise; but they laid firmly and deeply the foundation for the social and moral elevation of our people to-day. It is not the civilization of Paris and of Berlin that we wish to establish through the prayers and contributions of Christian men and women in this country, and the labours and sacrifices of our missionaries abroad, but rather one that may more nearly resemble in its spirit that of New England, while true in its forms to the genius of each people among whom we labour.

Our first work is to bring men to Christ, and then to introduce them to all the arts and accomplishments of true Christian culture. It is no easy matter to withstand the pressure of those who are eager for the material results of culture, who seek a high education, not to honour Christ, but to improve their social condition and worldly prospects. We could easily spend all our funds in Turkey alone in building up great institutions of learning and promoting the cause of science and the arts, and splendid material results might follow, but with them the infidelity and scepticism of France and the rationalism of Germany; and the establishment of the kingdom of Christ would be farther off than ever.

We carry everywhere the Bible and the school. The first book we would have read is the Bible, the first influence exerted that of the Gospel, to mould the religious character. We would rouse up a spirit among the people to seek for themselves the advantages of civilized and cultured life, and render them such aid and counsel as may be necessary at the start. In this view we seek first of all to raise up an educated ministry, who shall not be so far in advance of the people as to be out of sympathy with them, and whose habits of life should not lead to expenses above the present ability of their people to supply. The great centres in Turkey as in this country will require men of higher culture than the rural sections, and such men must be supplied. We are, therefore, raising the standard of education in our seminaries every year, and propose to keep them in advance of the growing intelligence of the people. Individuals of special gifts and ability will seek still further attainments by private studies under the advice of the older missionaries, and thus become prepared for the highest positions. Any other course than this will tend to keep your Churches dependent upon foreign aid, and perpetuate occasions for differences of feeling, and to give Protestantism the appliance of a foreign religion. It is now becoming naturalized, it is already a recognized national religion in the country, and any appearance of dependence in pecuniary or ecclesiastical matters should cease as soon as possible. For that result we are steadily striving, and desire to make ourselves unnecessary to the progress of the Gospel in Turkey at the earliest moment, and to see the Reformed Armenian Church standing forth in its might, a power for Christ. Then will our joy be fulfilled.

In this view we have welcomed the establishment of Evangelical Unions, and have desired to pass over into their hands, as far as possible, the entire conduct of their ecclesiastical affairs. The manner in which these responsibilities have been assumed is worthy of all praise,

and is full of promises for the future of the Church. As fast as the
Churches become independent we withdraw and leave them to the full
and free exercise of all their rights and liberties as Churches of Christ.
The proper missionary work—the extending of evangelistic labours
into new fields, and the grants in aid of feeble Churches toward the
support of their schools and preachers—belong to us; and in this we
seek the hearty co-operation of all who love our Lord. While we
desire the aid and counsel of our Armenian brethren in these plans,
the control of our funds is properly in our hands. This arrangement
is most satisfactory to our Churches at home, and saves complication
abroad. The wise and responsible use of funds necessitates careful
inquiry into the character of the objects for which they are appro-
priated, and may thus lead to temporary differences of judgment
between the missionaries and the Armenians on practical questions,
and sometimes to the appearance of interference in the local affairs
of the Churches. But it is a necessity that passes away with the
occasion, and ought to be promotive of good feeling rather than
otherwise.

The views I have thus set before you in this informal manner are
not peculiar to the American Board and its missionaries; but, so far
as I know, are accepted as the result of large experience and observation by nearly all or quite all of the great missionary societies of the
world, though individual missionaries here and there may dissent. This
very morning my eye has fallen upon a passage in the annual report
of the London Missionary Society, presented at its recent anniversary
in London, which expresses so perfectly what I would say of every
Church formed by our missionaries that I beg to call your attention
to it: "In its outward form it may be purely native to the lands in
which it flourishes. Though founded by friendly foreigners it need
not perpetuate the Western customs of the men who began it; but
native in its fellowship, its worship, and its action, its outward forms
shall more truly express and develop the feeling, the principle, and the
life of its Christian members than any foreign system can do. In a
word, pure in its spirit, complete in its consecration, filled with the
rich experience of the varied past, the full force of all its native elements shall be offered with simplicity and truth to the Saviour, who
is its Lord. This is the end to which the efforts, the co-operation, the
full Scripture teaching of all branches of the Church of Christ lead
us on."

I have thus, my dear Sir, written you quite at length, out of the high
respect we all entertain for you, and feeling that your acquaintance
with this country and our institutions would enable you the better to
understand our position.

The condition of our work at Constantinople has been a source of great anxiety to me for years; the want of harmonious co-operation between the missionaries and the Churches, the frequent misunderstandings that arise, have been quite inexplicable on any Christian grounds. I cannot help feeling that evil influences have been at work to disturb the peace and good feeling of the Christian community. Precisely what they are, and what measures should be taken to meet them, I am unable to determine. I hear that you are purposing to visit this country during the present season. If so, I shall hope to have the pleasure of a full and free conference with you on many points relating to the progress of the Gospel in Turkey. In the meantime, we trust your good offices will be employed to secure the restoration of peace and harmony in the Christian community. Your position and influence are such as to give especial weight to whatever you may do in behalf of good order and the progress of Christian culture.

With great respect, yours sincerely,

N. G. CLARK.

(As an *individual; not* in the name of
the Prudential Committee.)

To the Prudential Committee of the American Board at Boston,
Mass., U.S.A.

OSTEND, July 24, 1869.

CHRISTIAN FRIENDS,—On my leaving Constantinople, the 14th of May last, the quarrel between your missionaries there and the Evangelical Armenian community was at its height—the former, in the name and in behalf of the American Board, prosecuting, and the latter defending themselves, in public Turkish tribunal. All my previous efforts to bring about a better and a Christian understanding between these opposing parties not only failed, but was made the occasion of, by your missionaries, to bring odium on my personal character. Yet the interests at jeopardy in those quarrels being most momentous, and being dearest to me, as they doubtless are to the Christian heart everywhere, I was still desirous to find an expediency by which time might be given to the enraged passions of the parties to cool. It was then that the thought occurred to me that you might do great good in this way, and very properly too, by requesting the missionaries to suspend the proceedings they had already commenced in your name, and bring the subject before you for a hearing.

With this view my message of the 20th of May was forwarded you, the acknowledgment of the receipt of which was received by me here the day before yesterday, in a letter of Dr. Clark, dated May 31st. Although I do feel thankful to Dr. Clark for doing me the favour of writing that long letter, and though the most of what he says is in entire harmony with my own views, still I must confess that I cannot see the relevance of the topics therein discussed to the subject of my telegram.

It surprises and deeply pains me, my Christian friends, to learn that, after the matter was brought before you so urgently, still you found it to be your duty to allow the missionaries to continue to pursue a course which in the judgment of ninety-nine per cent. of all Evangelical Armenians (not mentioning the number of foreign Christians and the large body of most honourable men of every nationality who were in sympathy with them in this matter) was most disastrous to the missionary cause in Turkey. Dr. Clark in his letter remarks: "The condition of our work at Constantinople has been a source of great anxiety to me for years." And so, truly, he has reason to have anxiety; but can the anxiety of American Christians in behalf of a people six thousand miles away be compared with the anxiety of that people in its own behalf? What alarms our intelligent Christian men in Turkey is, that whatever is and has for years been true for Constantinople, is already partially true for every mission station among the Armenians in Turkey; and unless the Christian world begin to pray to God—and we were sure such a prayer would be answered—that He would keep back from the interior of Turkey, for fifty years at least, the great tide of education and intelligence which is so rapidly flowing in now, it will be wholly true very soon. And would not such a spectacle (may God divert it!) burn the heart of every true Christian?

Gentlemen, on these things you have the testimony of the missionaries alone. That is not enough. You must hear also whatever intelligent Armenian Christians have to say about them. They are most vitally interested in these affairs, and if they are refused to be heard, the cause of Christ in Turkey will sustain irreparable injury.

In Turkey, among the Armenians, the American Board had a most fruitful field for missionary labour, and hitherto God has blessed that labour. Still the work is yet by no means done as it ought to be done. To do it properly and well we must give up some of our prejudices. We must observe the signs of the times, and be willing to learn something from the world. Now, what are the signs of the times I refer to. Reform and liberty !!! Hitherto the missionaries have ruled like unconstitutional monarchs; and perhaps that way answered well in those days, but it will not answer now. Hitherto the Churches have been under the complete control of the missionaries as our American slaves were under the control of their masters; and perhaps that state of things was a necessity then, but surely it is not so now.

In one word, if you wish to see peace and prosperity in the missions in Turkey, curtail some of the powers of your missionaries, and break off some of the links from the chain that has been binding the Churches ever since their organization. Never allow any missionaries to be put to rule over persons who are not only superior to himself in age, but also in Christian experience, and many other talents. Although your missionaries are now unanimous in defending what was done on their side, yet I verily believe the recent crisis would have been diverted if older, calmer, and more experienced men were at the immediate head in the management of the affairs.

I have written thus, dear friends, as a Christian man, frankly, though very briefly and imperfectly, and pray that it may be read in the same spirit in which it was written. . . . .

S. M. MINASIAN.

To the Prudential Committee of the American Board, Boston, U.S.A.

OSTEND, BELGIUM, Aug. 6, 1869.

DEAR BRETHREN,—Since I wrote you on the 24th ult., I have received two letters from the Churches in the neighbourhood of Constantinople, and believing that, at a time like this, you would be desirous of obtaining all the information you could in regard to the difficulties between the missionaries and the Churches, I take the liberty of translating and sending them to you, premising, however, that I take no responsibility in the matter beyond thus making myself the medium of transmission.

I remain most respectfully yours,

S. M. MINASIAN.

Mr. S. M. Minasian.

BAGHGEJICK, July 5, 1869.

DEAR BROTHER IN CHRIST,—As it is already known to you, for the past three years we have been without a minister of the Gospel to preach in our village, and therefore were deprived of the blessings and comforts which the Lord instituted should come through the preaching of the Gospel of Christ.

But now, we thank the Lord that He has been pleased to grant us a preacher in the person of brother Hohannes Bassian. This brother, having laboured among us for a couple of months, we thought best to engage for a year, and after that, if it pleased God, to settle him permanently as our pastor. We have also a teacher, who labours faithfully, we believe, for the spiritual as well as mental instruction of our children, so they may, through the blessing of God, become useful in the future.

For the present year, to support our preacher and teacher, we need 90*l.*; 60*l.* for the preacher, and 30*l.* for the teacher.

We tried to raise this amount without making application for it to any friends outside, and to this end our [brethren and sisters, all with one heart, laboured, and the result was 60*l.* only.

As it is well known to you, our principal business here is the raising of silk cocoons, which business for several years past, as also the present year, has not been successful, and it was on this account that our efforts to raise the entire 90*l.* ourselves have failed.

Besides this, we have to raise 10*l.* for contingent expenses, also 114 pa's for Government taxes.

While we were meditating over these circumstances, our brother Alexander, the Pastor of Adapazar Church, met us, and exhorted us not to be discouraged, reminding us that there were Christian friends, such as Rev. Dr. Hamlin and Mr. Minasian, who felt interested in us, and promised to aid us when we found a preacher.

Thus, dear brother, we are encouraged to apply to you to assist us in the support of the Gospel institution in this village, and hope our application will meet with your approval.

D

We also make known to you, with deep sorrow, that for several years there have been differences between the Rev. Mr. Parsons, the missionary of the American Board here, and ourselves, concerning the manner of working for spreading the kingdom of Christ in our midst. We applied to the Missionary Committee at Constantinople to send one here to investigate the matter, and mark out a course in which we can all work together in harmony. But the Committee at Constantinople have not given any importance to our application. We therefore thought it best, feeble though we are, to work alone, and independently of the missionaries in the kingdom of God in this land, hoping and praying that the Lord may strengthen us for His glory.

With earnest prayer we remain, yours, in behalf of all Evangelical Armenians at Baghgejick.

MINAS SEPETJIAN, TOROS MINASIAN, VAHAN DAIYAN, GARABED SINASIAN, HOHANNES TAVITIAN.	Committee of the Church.
HOHANNES CANDANIAN, SDEPHAN TOPOOSIAN, SARKIS PANOSIAN, SDEPHAN ARABIAN, HARGOP GOBELIAN.	Committee of the Society.

Mr. S. M. Minasian.

RODOSTO, July 17, 1869.

DEAR SIR,—On the 3rd inst. there arrived here the missionaries, Rev. Messrs. Schauffler and Baldwin, and on the 8th they returned to Constantinople. During the stay of these brethren with us we treated them with all the hospitality, civility, and kindness possible.

They first spoke privately with me and a few brethren, and laboured hard with threats and promises to induce us to repudiate the action of the Ecclesiastical Council convened at Constantinople the 19th of April last, and also to disapprove the letter sent by that Council to the Prudential Committee. But to do this we considered wrong, and contrary to our conscience.

In the evening of the 6th instant, the missionaries begged me to call a general meeting of the Church, which I did; but only seven members (that is only the half of the Church) being present, of course no business could be lawfully transacted, and so our brethren declared to the missionaries. But they persisted in their efforts to persuade the brethren present to act as a lawful meeting, and repudiate the action of the Council above referred to, and recall the letter to the Prudential Committee; but the brethren evidently opposed them, saying there is not a quorum present for transacting business, and as to repudiating the action of the Constantinople Council, it is childish, wrong, and against our conscience. Finding that they could accomplish nothing in this way, the young missionaries became angry, and venting the severity of their anger on myself, gave, in a paper signed by Mr. Schauffler, the following condemnatory decision in regard to myself:

" The mind of Pastor Abraham, in regard to our missionary work, policy, and principles, is so much at enmity, and his want of confidence in us is so great, that before it becomes altogether changed we hasten to declare that we cannot have intercourse with him as missionaries any longer; and that in regard to his salary we will not be able to assist.

" H. SCHAUFFLER."

Against this action I sent a protest to the Missionary Committee *ad interim* at Constantinople, of which I send you a copy, and beg that you will be pleased to draw the attention of American Christians to the grievous wrongs done to a poor minister of the Gospel of Christ in Turkey. Our Church and brethren unite with me in regards to you.

I remain sincerely yours,

PASTOR ABRAHAM.

Another friend at Constantinople writes: " Letters from Nicomidia this week mention that Mr. Parsons presented a paper to the Church there, requesting them to sign it, repudiating certain articles published in regard to the missionaries, otherwise all assistance to them will be cut off. The same thing was done to the Church at Rodosto."

S. M. Minasian, Esq.

MISSIONARY HOUSE, BOSTON, August 13, 1869.

MY DEAR SIR,—Your favour of July 24 has come to hand. I am sorry to find that our action and the contents of my letter are not agreeable to you. In regard to your telegram, I ought to say that we did not understand its purport till your letter came, and it was then too late to stay proceedings in the courts, even if we had thought it best to do so. As the result showed, the seizure of our property was an unjustifiable act of violence on the part of a portion of the Vlanga Church, and it could only have delayed justice to have had any interposition on our part.

The tyranny of which you complain is something I do not understand. The object of the missionary at any point is to develop and establish an independent, self-supporting, self-governing Church, and then to leave it to itself and go elsewhere. His power and authority cease the moment the Church is able to take care of itself. While it depends on him for the support of its pastor or its schools, it is but just that he should have a voice in its affairs, and not expend money for men or schools which he does not approve of. He will advise with the people and consult their wishes so far as possible. He will put all the responsibilities on them he can in order to prepare them to act for themselves just as soon as possible. This is our policy, and so we instruct all our missionaries. How such difficulty can arise as at Constantinople is a great surprise to me.

Will you have the kindness to tell me just what you want—just what manner of conducting the missionary work would please you and those who sympathize with you, and are opposed to the missionaries?

You complain bitterly, but I really do not know what you want. Excuse my frankness, but I am anxious for light.

Sincerely yours,

N. C. CLARK.

To the Prudential Committee of the A.B., Mission House, Boston, Mass., U.S.A.

PARIS, September 2, 1869.

DEAR FRIENDS,—The last note which I addressed you was dated August 6. Since then, a few days ago, I had the pleasure of receiving your favour of the 13th August. You wish me to state to you " just what manner of conducting the missionary work would please me and those who sympathize with me." I fear you do not understand exactly the nature of the relation I sustain towards the missionaries and the people among whom they labour.

I always prided myself that I belonged to neither party, and thought that my peculiar position enabled me to see the errors as well as the excellencies of both. It is not I who am discontented with the manner in which the missionary work is conducted—the people sympathizing with me, as you suppose, for the acts of the missionaries can in no wise affect me; but it is _the people_ who feel themselves oppressed and wronged by their acts. The expression of those feelings may be found in the frequent commotions between the missionaries and the Churches ;

the more intelligence in the Church, the louder and more frequent the complaint. My frequent opportunities of observation convince me that in this thing they are right; and must I suppress or withhold my sympathy from a people in that condition? It will be " woe " unto me if I do.

It requires a free talk and various explanations to make the state of affairs somewhat plain ; but as we have not that opportunity now, and as you are "anxious for light," I take the liberty to present the following statements on the subject : —

First. In the recent controversy with the missionaries I had *only one issue* with them, and that was on a most vital principle—the freedom of the Churches from outside interference—a principle absolutely indispensable for making the Evangelical Churches throughout Turkey self-supporting and self-propagating, and the violation of which, no matter on what grounds, and with what amount of pure and good motives, will bring distortion over those Churches; and thence the great end aimed at by the Christian Churches of America, with much prayer, through forty years of patient, faithful, and self-denying labours, and with the expenditure of much treasure, will fail to be accomplished. It would be far better for the Churches to be entirely free and make many mistakes than to be interfered with. It is always between two evils men have to choose in this imperfect world. It may seem presumptuous in me to speak of freedom to the free Churches of America. Yet, after being a most close observer of, and a most deeply interested party for more than twenty-five years in, what has been going on in connexion with the missionary work in Turkey. I cannot speak differently.

Second. The course pursued by your missionaries is in violation of just this principle spoken of. They virtually say to the needy Churches : " Obey us, and do as we say, even to the selection of your pastor, else we do not help you." But in the recent case not only did they say this to the Vlanga Church, but went beyond it. Several months before Pastor Sdepan was elected to have the temporary charge of the Vlanga Church, he started a meeting at Ortakeuy, one of the most important suburbs of Constantinople of a very large Armenian population, where any missionary work had never before been done. One day he invited all the missionaries of Constantinople, besides the Rev. I. G. Bliss, Dr. Hamlin, and myself, to a meeting to advise whether it was best for him to continue to labour at Ortakeuy, and whether the Mission or individual Christians would sustain him pecuniarily in that work, or to receive any other advice the meeting might give him. The meeting was convened ; the Rev. Messrs. Riggs, Bliss, Trowbridge, Hamlin, and myself, being present, and, after some deliberation, gave to Pastor Sdepan substantially the following advice :—

" The Mission, in times past, hired individuals to labour as evangelists in certain localities; but that plan is now abandoned, the present plan being to help the Churches, and let them undertake to do the missionary work of their districts. But as to yourself, there are the Vlanga and Adrianople Churches, both in need of a pastor; you may go to them and see, perhaps they will give you a call." It seems, however, that several members of the Vlanga Church were already at this time trying to persuade him to accept a call from their Church if it were offered him.

These brethren, who I understand take sides now with the missionaries, unanimously voted with the Church for Pastor S., and up to the last were among his most ardent supporters. It is further testified that some time previous the missionaries, in urging the Vlanga Church to call a pastor, suggested among other candidates Pastor Sdepan. But when the Vlanga Church, in a regular meeting, by a unanimous vote, elected Pastor S., and notice of it was given to the missionaries, they sent word to the Church to the following effect—viz.: " We decline to assist you to support Pastor S., because we are well convinced that his labours over the Churches of this capital will not be productive of good, and that our co-operation with him will be impossible."

This message was not taken very pleasantly by the Church, and she began to show signs of insubordination. But still, had the missionaries stopped there, the thing might have been arranged and the crisis averted; but they were inconsiderate, and went beyond, and when the Church, after considering their message, informed them that they had concluded to take the entire responsibility of the support of their pastor upon themselves rather than give up their choice, the missionaries brought a further and entirely unexpected pressure upon her in order thus to compel her to submit, saying: " The Vlanga Chapel is our property, and no man has the right to preach there without our consent. We do not consent to the preaching of Pastor S. there." At the same time they applied to the civil authorities to keep Pastor S. from entering the chapel. The civil authorities considered it beyond the range of their power or duty to interfere in keeping a man from peaceably entering a church edifice opened for public service, much less to prevent a minister from entering the edifice where his Church is assembled; but, wishing to make peace, proposed to have a neutral person preach until the matter between the parties could be amicably arranged.

But the missionaries would not consent to this, because Pastor S· would be present in the chapel as a mere hearer. I may here remark that the men of Turkey, though we might wish them to be, are not exceptions to, but of like passions with men everywhere. It was a wrong accusation the missionaries brought forward that the people were seizing their property. The Vlanga Church, in concert with the Protestant community in and around Constantinople, merely acted on the principle that they had the right to continue to hold their services in the chapel which they had been occupying by a common consent for the last seventeen years, until they received proper notice and time to quit. But the missionaries, instead of giving this notice, hastily, and without any warning, repaired to the place, discharged the people's school, nailed up the schoolroom, removed the family from the premises against their entreaties, called in the police to take away from the chapel a man who happened to be there, and locked up the building ; and, when they were remonstrated with for acting so rashly and unlawfully, declared, "We are foreigners, and not subject to Turkish law." Were they justified in thus acting? And were there no other considerations but the ownership of the property by which the Protestants of Stamboul, in the presence of their unsympathizing neighbours, could claim the right to be treated decently in this matter by the missionaries ?

Third. Turkey is not a missionary ground now in the sense that she was forty years ago. There is a people there now compared with which no other people in the world appreciate more the principles and privileges of the Gospel, to secure which they have been made to suffer " the loss of all things." To sustain and perpetuate the institution of that Gospel is not only their sincere desire, but it is also to their interest. In this work they have many wants, and they need ask the sympathy and aid of their more favoured fellow-Christians and the Christian Churches in other lands; being convinced and desirous, however, that aid should be granted on the simple ground of their being of the body of the Church of Christ, founded on his pure Gospel, and sincerely seeking to spread that Gospel, believing that their end, and the end of the Christians who help them, would be best secured if no other conditions were imposed upon them. The foreign missionary should never exercise " power and authority " over the Church because " it depends on him for the support of its pastor or its schools;" that is, not any more power than the home missionary exercises over feeble Churches in the West which he aids.

I have merely touched on the above points with the sincere desire to draw your patient and earnest attention to the grave questions under consideration ; and hoping that some means might be found by which harmony and co-operation between the missionaries and the Churches may be established, I remain, most respectfully, yours,

S. M. MINASIAN.

To the Prudential Committee of the A.B., Boston, Mass., U.S.A.

PARIS, November 5, 1869.

DEAR FRIENDS,—Since I addressed you my last communication I have received two letters, one from Pastor Thomas, of Diarbekir, and the other from Pastor Simon, of Constantinople; and I herewith take the liberty to send the translations of them to you, thinking that, considering their position and their labour in the missionary work in Turkey for a quarter of a century or more, you would be glad to have their views touching the state of that work.

I also enclose the copy of the letter I wrote to Rev. Mr. Washburn, at Constantinople, on receiving the report of the recent investigating committee there.

Respectfully yours,

S. M. MINASIAN.

P.S.—It is very much to be regretted that such an unguarded report* as I have just read was published by the A.B. concerning the recent difficulties at Constantinople. I presume that report was prepared before full and more correct information as to the actual causes and the nature of the difficulty had reached the Missionary House, otherwise the case would not have been so painfully misrepresented.

It not only does extreme injustice to earnest Christian men who honestly differed with the missionaries and remonstrated with them, but also does injury to the cause of truth and religion. For the sake of all I hope in some way it may be rectified.

S. M. M.

---

* *Extract from the Annual Report of the American Board,* 1869. — "At Constantinople the missionaries have been greatly tried by the conduct of a portion of the Protestant community. The motives and conduct of the missionaries in endeavouring to raise them to independence and to the support of their own institutions at the earliest practical moment have not been properly appreciated, and secret and open enemies of the truth have improved the occasion to embarrass our work. The experience of the early Churches as recorded in the Acts and the Epistles of the New Testament finds renewed and painful illustration at Constantinople. Happily, the difficulties thus referred to are thus far wholly confined to the capital and its immediate neighbourhood."

Mr. S. M. Minasian.

CONSTANTINOPLE, Oct. 8, 1869.

DEAR BROTHER IN CHRIST,—I need not describe to you now the recent events that have taken place here, as by this time you must have received sufficient information in regard to them. It is not possible to foretell what the effect of these events will be for the future, but thus far they have been injurious beyond measure, and if things continue in this way all hope for our work, at least in this capital, is terminated. Truly it has been a question of life and death to the Churches, and whatever little ray of light has been dimly shining has almost died out; and it only remains, it seems, for us to mourn in solitude over ourselves and our Churches, waiting for the omnipotent power of God to appear. Of course, this state of things has a double effect upon me. It is in itself a solemn and bitter thing to see scattered and in great danger the flock which God has committed to my unworthy care, and over which I have tenderly watched for the last twenty-five years, under circumstances of much trial and hardships of every kind.

Is it possible for a pastor to become a spectator of such a scene without having the greatest anguish of heart? Experience alone can answer the question.

This event has also a pecuniary effect of the hardest kind upon me.

I have spent more than a quarter of a century of my life in this work, all my powers, feelings, and desires have been nourished in it, and now I am compelled to give up this chosen work and calling, and at my present age run about like a young man of twenty in search of secular employment to support my wife and children. If it was an enemy who had given us this stroke it would certainly have been severe and unbearable; but now our hearts lie in more bitter and amazing sorrow because it was our brethren and our considered benefactors who have done it, those who were expressly sent to do us good, and from whom we certainly had the right to expect better things.

Alas! for the severe toils of many years. Alas! that the glorious cause of Christ, which had been secured only through a death-like struggle, has to be sacrificed to the passions of a few inexperienced men.

I have this painful news to communicate, dear brother, to you: the work for and in Constantinople is terminated.

May God save his cause in other places from coming to this most fearful and solemn end.

PASTOR SIMON.

S. M. Minasian, Esq.,

DIARBEKIR, September 9, 1869.

DEAR BROTHER,—Under the shadow of his wings, God has brought us safely home again. The brethren, about 2,000 in number, had come out of the city to meet us, and received us with great joy. Truly during these four years of separation their love for me had increased tenfold, notwithstanding the incessant efforts of the missionaries to induce them to discard me, saying to them that I would never return, or, if I did, would not be suited for them, &c., &c. The people were well convinced, however, that the cause of the opposition of the missionaries was that their Pastor did not obey them blindly; they would have the Church leave me and take such an one in my place as would submit to all their requirements without complaint. But now, as I have returned, they cannot find further fault with me on that ground, but still they seem determined to trouble this people and myself in another way. Our present meeting-house was purchased about ten years ago, for £1,000 Turkish, equal to 4,400 dollars. Of this amount the people here paid £300, of the balance the missionaries collected from Christians in America £420, and they also received from the funds of the American Board £280—the last-mentioned sum, however, was received as an advanced rent for use of the building by the Mission, and was to be liquidated by deducting from it so much every year as a rent. On my return here we wished the deeds of the premises, in order that we might commence our preparations to erect the new church edifice. They replied that they would not give it to us, unless we would pay for it. A few brethren and myself then went to see Mr. Williams and his associates, and tried to arrange the matter amicably with them. In order to settle the thing peaceably and harmoniously, we were willing to make even sacrifices if need be, and to this end offered to pay for their claim £150, in six equal annual instalments, with the endorsements of our brethren. To this arrangements Mr. Williams with his associates agreed perfectly, and seemed to feel rejoiced, too, that the matter was arranged in harmony and friendship, and said they would write to the missionaries at Kharpoot about it. They did so, and the answer was that they would not consent to the arrangement to give us the deeds unless we paid the £150 cash down. We applied again to Mr. Williams and the Kharpoot missionaries. It is now about six months since writing to the former, and it seems that they do not consider our letter even deserving an answer. From the Kharpoot missionaries we heard, and they answer as before, insisting on the payment of the £150 cash down, or we cannot have the deeds. They know very well that the brethren are not able to raise that amount for them now, as they will have to raise several hundred pounds before the building is finished, but still they persist in their demand, and in this way prevent us from commencing our work. While I was in America I was told that the buildings purchased for the people would be given to them; the same thing was repeated to me by the officers of the A.B. at the ministers' meeting at Dr. Crosby's house in New York. Now we are not asking any gift from the missionaries, we are offering payment and security, but they refuse to accommodate or give us their encouragement. Through all this summer we held our meetings in the open air, exposed to the heat and the dust, and now as the rainy season is approaching we know not where we can flee to. The present building is in an upper story 24 steps high, and far too small for the congregation, and I have fears also that it may some time give way, and endanger the lives of the people.

It seems strange to our people here that the missionaries should thus be the first to throw obstacles in the way, even before the Turks had commenced doing so. If you can find some way, through the Prudential Committee or otherwise, to deliver us from this embarrassing condition, you will accomplish great good. The condition of our people here is a difficult one. They raise annually more than £300 for their expenses, and considering their means, they all contribute liberally, and with much self-denial. Our work here is quite extensive, and in a few weeks the brethren are going to call in an assistant pastor. We have four schools; two—one for boys and one for girls—have recently opened, in which the higher branches of studies will be taught. In the boys' school the English and Turkish languages are also taught, and both schools are in a prosperous condition. It is hard to see so promising a field before us, and yet be prevented from fully entering into it for want of adequate means. We need school-books, maps, and various instruments, but cannot get them.

The missionaries in these parts, especially those of Kharpoot, are exercising extraordinary oppression over the people. Often, in order to continue to hold their rule over the Churches, they put uneducated and unsuitable persons as pastors over them, and in this way our people are falling into new kinds of errors and superstitions. I had often said, and am obliged to say still, that if things continue in this state these organized Churches will be ruined, and the missionaries with us all will view in sorrow their ruin.

I presume you have heard of the result of the recent events at Constantinople.

The missionaries say there is no work in Constantinople.

There are three Churches there, with each of which they are quarrelling. Let us pray that God may come to the rescue of his glorious cause.

I remain, sincerely yours, &c.,

PASTOR THOMAS.

Rev. G. Washburn.

PARIS, September 19, 1869.

DEAR BROTHER,—I am really glad for the turn the affairs in Constantinople have lately taken. The recent conference between the missionaries and the Churches, and the appointment of the commission to investigate the difficulties, were certainly steps towards important reform long needed.

I would also, as the commission did, express thanksgiving for the calmness and brotherly courtesy with which its deliberations were characterized, and for the impartiality and consideration, too, with which its opinions were declared and its recommendations made. I trust the improvement thus begun in the mutual relation between the missionaries and the Churches will be gradually extended, so that the evangelical work throughout Turkey may keep pace with the increasing intelligence and otherwise changed and reformed condition of the country. The long-existing state of the affairs in connexion with the missionary work in Turkey, as you know, has often been to many of the best friends of the cause of Christ there a cause of query whether Protestantism as a distinct organization should be longer kept up, and also if the ascendancy gained in the religious reformation in Turkey by the Christian Churches of America would or should longer continue. If we must take the affirmative side of these queries, it would necessitate the introduction of some important changes in the mode of missionary operations in Turkey.

The status of the native labourer with the missionary must be raised, his importance and equality to the missionary in the work must be practically acknowledged. The missionary should not be able to say to a native pastor, who, feeling his ministerial character injured by the former's official acts, appeals to him for redress: " There is no hope of redress for you this side of the water—as for my official acts, even if they injure your character, I am responsible only to my Board, six thousand miles away." Neither should he be again permitted to say to a Church: "Your pastor or delegate in an Ecclesiastical Council of your sister Churches voted unfavourably to us, therefore you must repudiate his acts, else, as we are the keepers and distributors of the money, we cannot conscientiously assist you to sustain the institution of the Gospel in your midst."

This state of things ought to be changed, and I trust, as the commission respectfully recommends, the American Board will send " a deputation to Turkey to visit the Churches, confer personally with the brethren, examine the present state of the work, and fix upon the principles upon which the missionaries and the Churches are to labour together."

I am not in favour of inciting a subject people to opposition, yet I hold that when they want or ask for liberty it must be granted. The very fact of their asking for it proves that they appreciate and are prepared to enjoy it. May God grant us all the spirit of humility, so that we may daily ask, " Lord, what wilt thou have me to do ?"

I remain, yours, &c.,

S. M. MINASIAN.